RESTLESS RIVER

International Law and the Behavior of the Rio Grande

To my parents and to the memory of theirs.

Restless River

*International Law
and the Behavior
of the Rio Grande*

by

JERRY E. MUELLER

TEXAS WESTERN PRESS
THE UNIVERSITY OF TEXAS AT EL PASO

1975

F
786
.M945   {iv}

CONTENTS

ILLUSTRATIONS

TABLES

RESTLESS RIVER

International Law and the Behavior of the Rio Grande

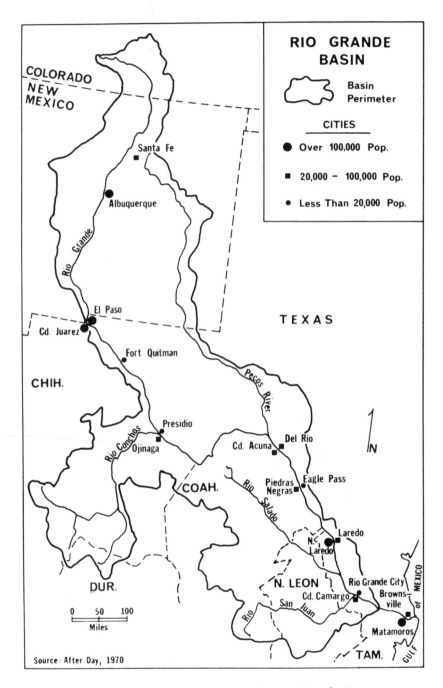

FIGURE I-1. *Orientation map of the Rio Grande Basin.*

I

Introduction to the Lower Rio Grande

❦ The Rio Grande heads in the glaciated San Juan Mountains of southwestern Colorado and flows south through a series of structural basins some 650 miles to El Paso, Texas. From El Paso, where the River becomes the international boundary between the United States and Mexico, the Rio Grande runs southeast another 1,250 miles and drains into the Gulf of Mexico near Brownsville, Texas.

A true exotic stream, like all major rivers of the arid zones, the Rio Grande is fed by spring snow melt in its headwaters, traverses desert through most of its length, eventually making its way to the sea with the aid of a few major tributaries and summer thunderstorm runoff. Were it not for the high discharge received from the Rio Conchos at Ojinaga, Chihuahua, the Rio Grande would not be a perennial stream. Another major tributary is the Pecos River, which drains the east slope of the Rockies in southeastern New Mexico, severs the Stockton Plateau from the Edwards Plateau in West Texas, and joins the Rio Grande upstream of Del Rio. The Rio Salado drains the northern portion of the Mexican State of Nuevo Leon and joins the Rio Grande at Falcon Reservoir midway between Laredo and Rio Grande City. Just above Rio Grande City, the Rio San Juan contributes the discharge it collects from central Nuevo Leon (Fig. I-1).

Reservoir construction and irrigation in the last sixty years have reduced the Rio Grande's flow to only a fraction of pre-1900 discharges. The upper basin, defined here as that portion which lies north of El Paso and the international boundary, now has numerous dams and reservoirs and practically no spring flooding from snow melt; some minor flooding is associated with local summer thunderstorm runoff. At Fort Quitman, approximately 80 miles downstream of El Paso, mean annual discharge has been reduced by 95 percent as a result of reservoir storage and redistribution of waters in the upper basin.

Below its junction with the Conchos, the Rio Grande has not been harnessed as severely as it has in the El Paso area, although fresh-water loss to the Gulf of Mexico has lessened by approximately 87 percent. Flash flooding is much more prevalent along the lower Rio Grande than it is along the upper reaches of the River, and is usually associated with either summer convection storms or occasional tropical storms that move inland from the Gulf. A very large flood on the lower Rio Grande approaches 1,000,000 cubic feet per second discharge; a very large flood on the upper Rio Grande has only 25,000 cubic feet per second discharge (Day, 1970: 9-17).

There is considerable disagreement about the origin of the River's present course. Most authors have concluded that the Rio Grande originally flowed into the El Paso region and fanned out into a series of inland deltas or lakes. The Conchos is presumed to have drained into the Gulf via what is now the lower Rio Grande. Later, headward erosion by a Conchos tributary supposedly pirated the Rio Grande near El Paso during the Pleistocene and initiated a through-flowing system (Bryan, 1938 and Kottlowski, 1958). Recently there has been identified some stratigraphic and paleontological evidence that supports this view (Strain, 1966, 1970). The other view is that the Rio Grande has been through-flowing since its inception (Ruhe, 1962).

From El Paso to the Big Bend country, the River flows through the Open Basin Section of the Basin and Range Physiographic Province. The international boundary heads in El Paso where the River is narrow and pinched between the Cerro de Cristo Rey on the west and the foothills and fans of the Franklin Mountains to the east. Cristo Rey is a Cenozoic dome with an andesitic core and steeply dipping Cretaceous marine strata on the flanks. The gorge cut by the River in the beds at the base of Cristo Rey became the famous Pass to New Mexico for Spanish explorers of the sixteenth and seventeenth centuries (Sonnichsen, 1968: 4) (Fig. I-2).

The Franklin Mountain Range is a tilted horst that has been rotated sharply to the west. This north-south trending range of mountains is dominated by a thick sequence of Precambrian and Paleozoic sedimentary marine rocks, with some granites and rhyolites. It is the toe of the Franklins that extends far into the city of El Paso and around which the Rio Grande makes its bend to the southeast. Between El Paso and Big Bend the River flows on a floodplain of Recent alluvium flanked by fans and terraces of Pleistocene river deposits, except for local constrictions and greater entrenchment as it approaches the Bend.

FIGURE I-2. *Upstream view of the dissected base of Mt. Cristo Rey where Spanish explorers left the valley and swung westward around the mountain, returning to the River and a ford a few miles upstream.*

(Photo by the author.)

Physiographically, the Big Bend is the Great Bend Section of the Mexican Highlands Province. Here the River is contained in the great canyons it has cut across the complex folded, faulted, and intruded structures in thin Paleozoic and thick Mesozoic strata. Near the east edge of the Bend country, the Rio Grande traverses the southern extension of the Great Plains Province and flows parallel to the escarpment of the Stockton Plateau. Below its juncture with the Pecos, the River once again flows on Recent alluvium across the Gulf Coastal Plain, which is underlain by poorly consolidated Cenozoic strata (Maxwell and Dietrich, 1965).

Climate

Two ingredients account for the major differences in climate along the lower Rio Grande. The first, which follows the gradient of the River, is elevation; the second is the proximity of the Gulf of Mexico, a source of maritime tropical air (Table I-1). At El Paso-Juarez, 1,250 miles upstream from the Gulf, maritime air is rare and polar outbreaks from the north are infrequent. During most of the year the El Paso area is under the dominance of the desiccating, stable sector of the subtropical high pressure system. The climate here is typified by low annual precipitation, most of which is received from summer thunderstorms. Year-round low humidity produces large diurnal ranges in temperature, 30-40 deg. F. being common. Spring, usually the driest season, is characterized by the duststorms and sandstorms of March and April. The area is protected from summer heat extremes by its elevation of 3,800 feet. According to the Koeppen system, the El Paso-Juarez region classifies as having a BWh climate, that of a hot desert.[1]

---

[1] The boundary between desert and steppe (BW and BS climates) in the modified-Koeppen system for stations with no excessive seasonal concentration of precipitation is determined by r equals (.44t − 8.5)/2, where r equals mean annual precipitation and t equals mean annual temperature in degrees F. For El Paso the boundary is 9.81 inches. Therefore, the city classifies as a BW or desert climate because it receives on the average only 8.44 inches. A desert station with all mean monthly temperatures above 32 deg. F., such as El Paso, is designated as recording a BWh, or hot desert, climate.

TABLE I-1

Lower Rio Grande Climatic Data

	EL PASO	DEL RIO	BROWNSVILLE
Elevation	3,800 ft.	1,025 ft.	25 ft.
Mean Annual Temp. (deg.)	63.9 F.	69.7 F.	73.5 F.
Mean July Temp. (deg.	82.0 F.	85.2 F.	83.7 F.
Mean January Temp. (deg.)	44.8 F.	51.6 F.	60.3 F.
Record High Temp. (deg.)	106 F.	107 F.	104 F.
Record Low Temp. (deg.)	−8 F.	19 F.	19 F.
Days Above 90 deg. F.	104	130	97
Growing Season	205 days	290 days	330 days
Annual Precipitation	8.44 in.	18.03 in.	26.64 in.
Precipitation Regime	Summer max.	Summer max.	Summer max. Fall max.
Days with more than .01 in. Precipitation	44	53	71
Mean Noon Humidity in July	40%	46%	55%
Mean Noon Humidity in Jan.	40%	49%	65%
Annual Snowfall	5.0 in.	1.6 in.	trace
Evaporation From Free Water Surface	110 in.	115 in.	80 in.
Annual Sunshine	83%	70%	61%
Thunderstorm Days	38	35	26
Mean Wind Speed	9.8 Knots	9.6 Knots	12.0 Knots
Wind Direction	Summer-North Winter-South	Variable	Southeast

Source: U.S. Department of Commerce, 1970a, 1970b, 1970c; Orton, 1964: 159-63.

Del Rio, approximately midway between El Paso and Brownsville, overlooks the River at an elevation of 1,026 feet. Here the desiccating influence of the subtropical high lessens as it does near the east coast of all major continents. Therefore, maritime air from the Gulf is a more frequent visitor at Del Rio than it is at El Paso. Rainfall maximum occurs in summer in association with convective storms. There is also a strong orographic effect from the Balcones Escarpment to the north. The Del Rio area is classified as having a BSh, hot steppe, climate.[2]

[2] The boundary between humid and dry (B) climates is just double the rainfall boundary between desert and steppe climates. Del Rio requires between 11.08 inches and 22.17 inches of precipitation in order to classify as a BS steppe climate. Its mean annual precipitation of 18.03 inches and its relatively warm mean monthly temperatures designate the station as a BSh, or hot steppe, climate.

At Brownsville, a few miles inland from the Gulf, maritime air is dominant, although the subtropical high still controls most of the lower Rio Grande weather. Low elevations on the Coastal Plain behind Brownsville produce little orographic effect, and the moisture-laden maritime air is only occasionally lifted to the condensation level. Although classified as having a Caf, humid subtropical climate, Brownsville in fact receives just enough precipitation to escape classification as a BSh, hot steppe.[3] Two maxima of precipitation occur, one associated with mid-summer convective storms, the other with occasional hurricanes of September and October. The hurricanes, though infrequent, cause the climate to be classified as humid. Thus, Brownsville has a humid subtropical climate, but is characterized by subhumid steppe weather! (U.S. Department of Commerce, 1970a, 1970b, 1970c).

Ecology

The Chihuahuan Desert occupies north central Mexico and overlaps into the United States in southern New Mexico and southwest Texas. At El Paso the desert follows the River upstream into New Mexico and points like a large finger toward Albuquerque (Fig. I-3). In West Texas the desert occupies the lowlands below the terminus of the Rockies and extends as far east as Del Rio. The Chihuahuan Desert typically has fewer cacti species and individuals than the Sonoran Desert to the west. Adjacent to the Rio Grande, the desert is characterized by creosote bush, mesquite, cottonwood, agave, yucca, barrel cactus, salt bush, and sotol (Jaeger, 1957: 33-49).

Shelford includes this desert as part of the North American hot deserts, typified by the creosote bush-kangaroo rat biome. He divides the desert into two ecological sectors. Between El Paso and Del Rio north of the River, and between El Paso and the Rio Conchos south of the River, is the creosote bush-desert cottontail-yucca faciation.

3 According to the modified-Koeppen system, Brownsville classifies as a humid climate because its mean annual rainfall of 26.64 inches is greater than the city's humid-dry rainfall boundary of 23.84 inches. The station has a Caf, or humid subtropical, climate because its coldest mean monthly temperature is between 32 deg. F. and 64.4 deg. F. (C), its warmest month is above 71.6 deg. F. (Ca), and its rainfall is not seasonally concentrated (Caf).

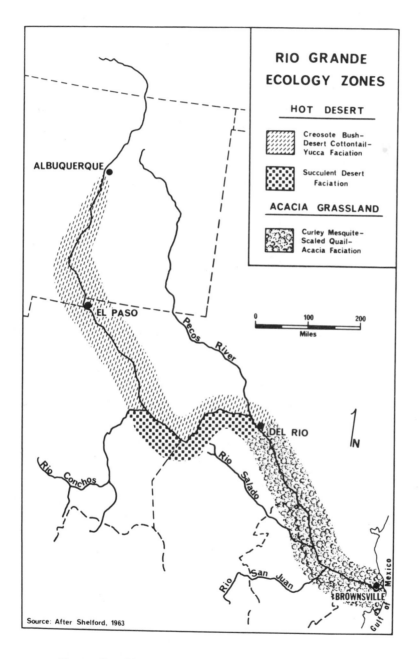

FIGURE I-3. *Map of Rio Grande Valley ecology zones.*

Characteristic plants include creosote bush, yucca, mesquite, agave, cacti, ocotillo, acacia, sotol, white thorn, and tar bush (Fig. I-4). Characteristic animals include cottontail rabbits, rattlesnakes, lizards, scaled quail, and mourning doves. On the Mexican side of the boundary, between the Rio Conchos-Rio Grande confluence and Del Rio, is the succulent desert faciation. Some typical plants are creosote bush, mesquite, agave, cacti, and tar bush, with grasses on the upland fringe. Common animals include rattlesnakes, cottontail rabbits, gophers, ground squirrels, and peccaries.

The ecology of the Rio Grande floodplain and tributary washes is quite different from that of the rest of the desert. Vegetation is dominated by cottonwood, desert willow, mesquite, acacia, reeds, and burrobush. Seep willows are the pioneer plants on freshly exposed river bars. Animal residents include rats, garter snakes, herons, and doves.

Downstream of Del Rio, the River transects the Acacia Grassland section of the Southern Temperate Grassland. Shelford calls this area the curley mesquite-scaled quail-acacia faciation of the grassland biome. Invasion of this area by shrubs from northern Mexico gives it an appearance of scrub land rather than of pure prairie or grassland. Common grasses are grama, wire, and three-awn. Shrubs include curley mesquite, mimosa, yucca (cenizo), gavia, macahinta, huisache, and prickly pear; palms occur at the Rio Grande Delta below Brownsville. Typical animals include three species of quail, doves, hawks, vultures, lizards, and bullsnakes (Shelford, 1963: 368-94).

History of Exploration and Settlement

The earliest record of contact with the Rio Grande by Europeans is 1519, when the Governor of Jamaica, Francisco Garay, ordered Captain Alonzo Alvarez de Pineda to command four unseaworthy ships and to find the water route to Cathay. While following the coast of the Gulf of Mexico in search of the passage, Captain Pineda anchored offshore at Veracruz, trespassing on Hernando Cortes' sphere of influence. Pineda sent several small boats ashore to make contact with Cortes, who replied with force and determination. Pineda's men scrambled for the mother vessels, pulled anchor, and sailed to the north. Repairs were soon needed, and the Captain ordered the ships anchored in safe near-shore waters where a palm-studded river delta fanned into the sea. Finding a pleasant physical setting and no problems with Indians during his stay of forty days, Captain Pineda returned to Jamaica and excitedly urged the Governor to colonize the area adjacent to the River. For many years to come, Spanish exploration journals were to speak of Pineda's Rio de las Palmas, our Rio Grande and the Mexicans' Rio Bravo del Norte.

The next year three ships left Jamaica under the command of Diego de Camargo, reached the River of Palms, and sailed approximately 20 miles upstream. Indians encamped along the River were apparently provoked by some of Camargo's men; the Indians retaliated, killed several Spaniards, and sent the fleet heading for the protection of the open sea. One ship was abandoned in mid-stream, another sank along the coast. The third ship, heavily laden with rescued personnel, sank as it approached Veracruz.

In 1523, Governor Garay personally commanded a contingency of sixteen ships and 750 soldiers whose object was to found a town at the River's mouth. Unable to find a suitable site, Garay decided to march south to the Rio Panuco and to reclaim the area from Cortes. In the meantime, Cortes received from Spain a royal grant to the area in dispute. When Garay learned of the grant, he peacefully joined Cortes' group and became politically inert under Cortes' domination (Horgan, 1954: 84-92).

The next major contact with the Rio Grande took place when Alvar Nunez Cabeza de Vaca, a sailor shipwrecked near Galveston in 1528, crossed Texas westward on foot and forded the River near what is now El Paso. By 1536 he made his way to Mexico City, carrying with him the golden city tales which had been passed on to him by the various Indians with whom he had traded.

Viceroy Don Antonio Mendoza had heard similar reports from other sources, and, as might be expected, organized a group, headed by Friar Marcos de Niza, to search for the legendary gold and silver in what is now New Mexico. The group found no gold, only pueblo Indians poor as peasants, but rich in more tales of golden cities.

By 1540 Viceroy Mendoza had organized another expedition, which was guided by Friar Marcos and headed by Francisco Vasquez de Coronado. Coronado's army marched on the Indians' golden city of Cibola, only to discover it was the Zuni Pueblo. Further embarrassment came when Coronado met an Indian called Turk, who talked day after day about Quivira to the east, the land of gold, silver, and large fish. After several forays into what is now the panhandle area yielded nothing, Turk was executed by Coronado's men, and the expedition returned to Mexico City (Steen, 1948: 2-6).

Decades passed before another expedition was sponsored. In the meantime, speculation arose that the large river into which the Rio Conchos drained was in fact the same Rio Grande previous parties had known in New Mexico. If so, then future expeditions could follow the Conchos to the Rio Grande, then follow the main river upstream to New Mexico. The principal route before 1580 was far to the west through Arizona country. In 1581, friars headed by Agustin Rodriquez and soldiers commanded by Francisco Sanchez Chamuscado

FIGURE I-4. *View of vegetation zones along the Rio Grande Valley near El Paso. Grasses dominate in the foreground where drainage on a section of old floodplain is poor. The squatty-looking trees behind the man are saltcedars (Tamarisk) that are found in abundance along the outermost edge of the floodplain. Foothills behind saltcedar are gravelly and well-drained, supporting a good cover of evergreen creosote bush. Franklin Mountains appear in background.* (Photo by the author.)

successfully followed the new Conchos route. In 1582, Antonio de Espejo explored the New Mexico area, and, very importantly, decided to take a more southerly return route to Mexico via the Pecos River. Evidence suggests he left the Pecos where it follows a southeasterly course, crossing overland to the Rio Grande near the site of present Presidio (Fig. I-5). Espejo could well have been the first European to make contact from the north with the middle reach of the River's lower course (Horgan, 1954: 154-56). Eight years later Gaspar Castano de Sosa explored the reach of the River between the mouths of the Pecos and Devils Rivers (Steen, 1948: 8).

He was the last of the Spanish explorers who reached the Rio Grande. All of them had started with visions of gold or of power, temporal or spiritual. All of them had found death or disgrace or both. But they had also found the way (Fergusson, 1955: 54).

In 1595 Don Juan de Onate was appointed governor of New Mexico and was commissioned to settle the territory. By 1598 his contingency forded the River at what was to become the site of El Paso del Norte (Juarez), crossing to the east bank, and continued into New Mexico.[4] Not only did Onate firmly establish the route between Old and New Mexico via El Paso, but he also shortened it considerably by going overland directly to the Pass. Onate ruled New Mexico until 1608, leaving behind several thriving settlements (Faulk, 1965: 32, 33).

Missions established to serve Indians and settlers along the Mexican frontier provided the nuclei around which the first permanent settlements were established along the lower Rio Grande. Guadalupe Mission in present Juarez was founded in 1659. With the Pueblo Revolt of 1680, numerous Indians and settlers left New Mexico and settled around the Guadalupe Mission. Many other missions were established in the succeeding decade, some to serve special groups, such as the Ysleta Mission designed in 1682 for the Tiguas. Another mission was founded in 1682 at Socorro, and several were established in the Presidio area in 1683-84.

---

[4] El Paso del Norte was renamed Ciudad Juarez in 1888 in honor of Mexican hero Benito Juarez.

Although Spanish authority was soon reinstated in New Mexico, there was little new development or settlement of the Rio Grande Valley between 1685-1746, largely because Spain was concerned with combating the French influence in East Texas. Initial settlement of what is now the lowermost Rio Grande took place between 1748-55 under the direction of Jose de Escandon. Escandon systematically founded twenty-three towns and fifteen missions. Most towns became centers of ranching, such as Camargo and Reynosa in 1749, Dolores and Revilla (Guerrero) in 1750, Mier, Roma, and Rio Grande City in 1753, and Laredo in 1755 (Scott, 1966: 25-47).

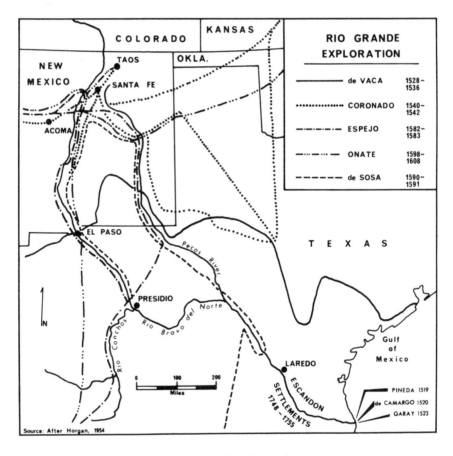

FIGURE I-5. *Map of Rio Grande exploration routes.*

By 1803, Louisiana had been twice exchanged between France and Spain, and ended up United States territory through the Louisiana Purchase. In 1821 Mexico received her independence; in 1836 Texas won hers. Since 1821 the settlement of the lower Rio Grande has occurred simultaneously from the United States to the north and from Mexico to the south. Most of this growth and development has been around previously established towns.

The lower Rio Grande has experienced two surges of settlement since the days of Escandon. One took place after the United States and Mexico established their boundary in 1848 and 1853. The second occurred after the arrival of the railroads in the 1870's and 1880's, especially at El Paso.

In 1970, there were approximately two million persons living in River towns from El Paso to the Gulf, with a slight majority on the Mexican side. Mexican towns have a population of nearly 100 percent Spanish surnames, while on the Texas side of the River the figure ranges between 58 percent at El Paso and 96 percent at Eagle Pass. The total population figures are deceiving because most people (nearly 70 percent) are concentrated in sister cities on the two sides of the border (Table I-2). Along most of the lower Rio Grande the population is exceedingly sparse. According to Horgan, the sister cities are bound by commerce, appetite, and corruption; but parted by language, boundary, and law (Horgan, 1970).

TABLE I-2

Population of Rio Grande Sister Cities in 1970

MEXICO		UNITED STATES	
CITY	POPULATION	CITY	POPULATION
Juarez	424,135	El Paso	322,261
Ojinaga	12,757	Presidio	930
Acuna	32,500	Del Rio	21,330
Piedras Negras	64,698	Eagle Pass	15,364
Nuevo Laredo	151,253	Laredo	69,024
Camargo	16,097	Rio Grande City	5,676
Matamoros	186,146	Brownsville	52,522

Source: U.S. Department of Commerce, 1971-1972; Vandertulip, 1974.

IMPORTANT SITES IN
THE RIO GRANDE
PRE-BOUNDARY ERA 1810-1848

EL PASO

RIO BRAVO DEL NORTE

NUECES RIVER

SAN JACINTO

TEXAS

CHIHUAHUA

MONTERREY

MATAMOROS

BUENA VISTA

M E X I C O

GULF
of
MEXICO

GUANAJUATO

GUADALAJARA

MEXICO CITY

VERA
CRUZ

PUEBLA

N

0   100   200
Miles

ACAPULCO

FIGURE II-1. *Map of important sites in the pre-boundary era.*

II

Events Prior to Fixing the River as Boundary

ω The impetus [force] for Mexican independence from Spain came in 1808 when Napoleon jailed King Ferdinand VII and smashed royalist forces. Details of the event reached New Spain in 1810. In Mexico there were factions of loyalists to both the deposed king and to the new junta, as well as to a third group eager to try for independence. Miguel Hidalgo y Costilla, a priest, was the first independence revolutionary, leading a revolt by unemployed Indian, Negro, and Casta miners at Guanajuato (Fig. II-1). The movement spread quickly, owing to the immediate capture of Guanajuato, and to the wide popular appeal of Hidalgo as the poor man's crusader.

Hidalgo moved his forces to Guadalajara where he set up his capital, abolished slavery, and published an independence newspaper. His forces were finally routed in 1811 by the loyalist army at Puente de Calderon. Hidalgo escaped and headed for the United States, only to be captured at Chihuahua and executed.

The rebellion was reorganized in 1812 by Jose Maria Morelos, whose principal achievement was the capture of Acapulco. In the meantime a new Spanish constitution was issued which included some of the reforms sought by the rebels. Interest in the movement waned until Morelos declared Mexican independence in 1813. Finally, in 1814, Morelos was captured after losing a battle to Colonel Agustin de Iturbide; in 1815 Morelos was executed (Hasbrouck, 1963: 489-94).

In 1820 the two major powers in Mexico were the Criollos (American born Europeans) and the Church. Both opposed the new regime of the Spanish Revolution and its religious reforms. Meanwhile, Vincente Guerrero, a follower of Morelos, had rejuvenated the revolt with his band of guerrillas. Viceroy Apodaca immediately called Iturbide out of retirement to suppress the revolt, the same Iturbide who had defeated Morelos a few years before. Unknown to the Viceroy, the loyalist commander had become convinced during the intervening years that the Criollos would support an independent Mexican monarchy. Instead of engaging in great battle, Iturbide and Guerrero met in 1821 and shaped their Plan of Iguala. They agreed on Mexican independence under a constitutional monarchy to be headed by Ferdinand VII or another European prince. Elimination of race distinction and the authorization of the Catholic Church as the national religious body were also agreed upon.

Iturbide, eager to effect the Plan, intercepted Spain's newly appointed Viceroy, Juan O'Donojo, who was on his way to Mexico City from Veracruz. The Plan was accepted and Iturbide went on to the capital as head of the junta government. His government was soon replaced by a regency that ruled until 1822. In that year the Viceroy died and Iturbide learned that Spain had officially rejected his Plan of Iguala; he then had himself proclaimed emperor. From its inception the new government was nearly bankrupt, and there was much dissention due to Iturbide's selfish bypassing of the Plan. Iturbide abdicated in 1823 and Mexico became a federal republic in 1824. Iturbide succeeded in securing independence, but also fostered a sequence of unstable governments that were unable to withstand the expansionist pressures of the United States (Davis, 1968: 322-27).

Texan Independence, 1836

Just prior to the Spanish Revolution of 1820, Stephen Austin arranged with the Spanish Crown to settle portions of Texas with Anglos. His request had to be renewed with newly independent Mexico, who not only granted permission, but also encouraged Anglo settlements. The economy of the new settlements was entirely based on cattle and cotton, the latter of which was dependent on slavery. By 1829 Mexico had abolished slavery and much pressure was placed on the Texas cotton industry.

Texas could either submit to national law or defy the emancipation and attempt to gain her independence. The latter route was chosen in 1835 when general revolt broke out against Santa Anna in Mexico, and when Texas Anglos outnumbered Texas Mexicans by nearly eight to one. Santa Anna personally commanded Mexican forces to suppress the Texas revolt and was initially successful. He was finally defeated in 1836 at San Jacinto, where he promised to get Mexican recognition of independent Texas, a course of action he never undertook.

At the same time, Sam Houston, the Texas leader, turned to Washington and requested immediate recognition of Texas as an independent republic, or annexation of Texas to the United States. President Jackson, while sympathetic, turned the matter over to Congress after being influenced by anti-slavery groups in the United States and by the Mexican Government itself. Congress granted Texas recognition as the Lone Star Republic, but defeated a bill for Texas annexation in 1838 (Davis, 1968: 440-42).

Texas Annexation 1845

Most European countries followed suit and recognized Texan independence. Britain did not. Instead, she sought in Texas a buffer against further United States expansion, i.e., Manifest Destiny. Texas wooed Britain in an effort to force annexation on the United States. The United States, fearing a British Protectorate in Texas, invoked the Monroe Doctrine.

At the time of the United States presidential election of 1844, expansionism had already displaced slavery as the country's main political issue. James Polk campaigned for Manifest Destiny, including the reoccupation of Oregon and the annexation of Texas. Following Polk's election, Congress voted its approval of annexation. Meanwhile, Britain had arranged for Mexican recognition of Texan independence. In return, Texas promised to abolish slave trade and to annex to no other country. Thus, Texas had a choice of annexing to the United States and offending Mexico, or of becoming an independent British Protectorate and offending the United States. Her legislature voted annexation in 1845; United States war with Mexico was imminent (Conner, 1965: 225-34).

United States-Mexican War of 1846

War might have been averted had Polk not been greedy. His envoys to Mexico in 1845 were instructed to request Mexican recognition of the Texas annexation, in exchange for the cancellation of debts owed the United States. Mexico probably would have conceded had Polk not also asked to buy California.

Another problem arose which proved to stifle negotiations. Just what was Texas? It had taken much discussion and several treaties a few decades before to decide its northern boundary. Its southern boundary had never been delimited. Polk demanded the Rio Grande. The Mexicans were understandably furious. Had not Spanish explorers used the Rio Grande as a principal route? Had not Escandon settled the area on either side of the River a century before? Had not Anglo settlements under Austin been much further north?

Polk apparently did not consider these questions. General Zachary Taylor and his troops were sent to occupy the area between the Nueces River and the Rio Grande, and to repel any Mexican attempts to cross to the north side of the River. War officially began in 1846 with a battle at Matamoros. Santa Anna, in exile in Cuba, returned to power and led the Mexican Army.

During Santa Anna's absence, Mexico had become very weak politically and financially, due in large part to repeated revolutions. Despite some difficulty, General Taylor succeeded in capturing Santa Anna at Buena Vista and captured Monterrey in 1847. In the meantime, General Winfield Scott advanced at will after landing at Veracruz, taking Puebla and Mexico City. California had already been secured. Manual de la Pena y Pena became the head of the Mexican Government after Santa Anna's exile, and to him came the task of negotiating a settlement (Dufour, 1968: 171-84, 259-78).

Treaty of Guadalupe Hidalgo 1848

There was no doubt that the Rio Grande was about to form a very large segment of the international boundary between the United States and Mexico. Why were Polk and other expansionists obsessed with getting the River as boundary? In all likelihood, they looked upon the Rio Grande Valley as real estate that even they did not believe was part of Texas. Just as important is the fact that the Rio Grande already possessed an international charm. Charles V in 1525 claimed the Rio de las Palmas as the western boundary of Florida. In 1682 La Salle claimed all lands east of the River as French. Both France and Thomas Jefferson later claimed the Rio Grande as the boundary of Louisiana. Henry Clay in 1827 and President Jackson in 1833 tried to buy Texas and have the River designated as the international boundary. Polk simply reiterated earlier views and demands (Horgan, 1954: 780-81).

The treaty signed by the two countries at Guadalupe Hidalgo gave the United States all of New Mexico, Arizona, California, Nevada, Utah, and parts of Colorado and Wyoming. Mexico received $15 million and cancellation of her debts. The treaty also established the international boundary between the United States and Mexico. Article 5 reads as follows:

> The boundary line between the two republics shall commence in the Gulf of Mexico, three leagues from land, opposite the mouth of the Rio Grande, otherwise called Rio Bravo del Norte, or opposite the mouth of its deepest branch, if it should have more than one branch emptying directly into the sea; from thence, up the middle of that river, following the deepest channel, where it has more than one to the point where it strikes the southern boundary of New Mexico . . . (9 Stat. 922).

This treaty did not, as stated by some authors, simply set the boundary in the middle of the River (Hovel, 1960: 1). Had it done so, the task of surveying the boundary would have been entirely non-fluvial, with markers placed periodically midway between the river banks or valley walls. Instead, the treaty designated the channel of maximum depth as boundary along those reaches where the River had more than one channel. Although used sparingly along the Rio Grande and not mentioned specifically by name in this or any other United States-Mexican treaty, such practice of marking the deepest channel is commonly referred to in international law as "the Principle of Thalweg." In alluvial streams such as the Rio Grande, the thalweg channel shifts position in time and place in response to varying flow regimes. Therefore, was the boundary as designated by the treaty fixed in time and place, or in neither? Would the river remain the boundary in the event of a meander cutoff?

These and similar questions cannot be answered from the text of the treaty itself. No provisions were made for a wandering thalweg. This circumstance was in part due to the hastiness with which the treaty was fashioned and signed; a large part was due to ignorance of alluvial river behavior.

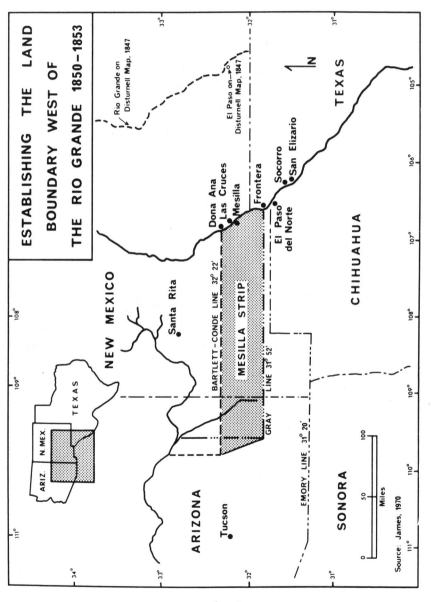

FIGURE III-1. *Fixing the land boundary west of the Rio Grande.*

III

Fixing the Boundary 1849-1855

W The Treaty of Guadalupe Hidalgo provided for an international boundary of four segments, two by land and two by water. By far the longest segment is the Rio Grande. Such a water boundary is generally not too difficult to demarcate. A surveyor merely needs astronomical readings from which he can determine the latitude and longitude of selected stations along the river bank. It is then possible to record positions in the middle of the deepest channel by triangulation from the bank positions. A major problem is to determine the thalweg channel in rivers like the Rio Grande where multiple channels are common.

To run a survey over land requires some original points for which the grid coordinates are given or can be determined. Intermediate positions are then found to shorten the gaps along the traverse. A case in point is the land traverse from where the international boundary leaves the River near El Paso. According to the treaty, this line was to run west from the point where the River strikes the southern boundary of New Mexico. According to Article 5,

The southern and western limits of New Mexico, mentioned in this article, are those laid down in the map, entitled "Map of the United Mexican States, as organized and defined by various acts of the Congress of said republic, and constructed according to the best authorities. Revised edition. Published at New York, in 1847, by J. Disturnell"; of which map a copy is added to this treaty, bearing the signatures and seals of the undersigned plenipotentiaries . . . (9 Stat. 922).

Both countries agreed that a joint boundary commission was necessary to implement the boundary as described in the treaty. Article 5 states that:

. . . the two Governments shall each appoint a commissioner and a surveyor, who, before the expiration of one year from the date of the exchange of ratifications of this treaty, shall meet at the port of San Diego, and proceed to run and mark the said boundary in its whole course to the mouth of the Rio Bravo del Norte. . . . The boundary line established by this article shall be religiously respected by each of the two republics, and no change shall ever be made therein, except by the express and free consent of both nations, . . . (9 Stat. 922).

Weller Commission

Polk's first commissioner died within a month of his appointment. John Weller was appointed the new commissioner, with Andrew Gray as surveyor and Major William Emory as chief astronomer and escort commander. In July, 1849 the commission met the Mexican Commissioner General Conde and his surveyor Major Salazar at San Diego. At the same time, the incoming Whig administration of President Taylor decided to replace the Democrat Weller.

Fremont Commission

The Whig's new commissioner was John Fremont, who had just recently been ousted from the military by court-martial. During the six months it took Fremont to reach California, Weller went ahead with the survey at San Diego and ran the line east to the Gila River. Weller then adjourned the commission, returned to California, and got elected as Democratic senator of the new state. Not to be outdone, Fremont arrived in California and shortly thereafter became the state's second senator. The frustrated Major Emory resigned from the commission, leaving only surveyor Gray to represent the United States.

Bartlett Commission

Another commission was designated in 1850 with John Bartlett, a Rhode Island book dealer, appointed commissioner. Gray was retained as surveyor, and John McClellan was hired to replace Emory as chief astronomer. Bartlett was the epitome of the spoils system, bringing with him no qualifications whatsoever. Neither was he a man of simple taste. His entourage would be outfitted with the best equipment; government funds financed his luxurious dining and side trips. While Bartlett's 105 commission appointees, including tailors and servants, sailed directly from New York to Indianola on the Texas Gulf, the commissioner and his staff took side trips to Havana and New Orleans, arriving in Indianola a full week later than the commission's main force. Bartlett's rockaway coach finally reached El Paso on November 13, 1850, ten days after the first scheduled meeting of the commissioners. Not until December 2, 1850 did the joint commission meet (James, 1970: 26).

In the midst of planning their surveys, the commissioners discovered one of the most noteworthy cartographic errors in history. Disturnell's map showed El Paso del Norte (Juarez) at 32 deg., 15 min. north latitude, when it is actually at 31 deg., 45 min., or approximately 34 miles farther south (Fig. III-1). The city's longitude was given as 104 deg., 39 min. west, when in fact it is 106 deg., 29 min., or approximately 130 miles farther west. The question arose as to whether or not the boundary should leave the River at 8 miles above Juarez, as shown on the map, or 42 miles above Juarez, as indicated by the incorrect grid.

Mexico would have gained territory by having the boundary run west from a point in the Mesilla Valley 42 miles upstream of Juarez. Commissioner Conde proposed that since the Disturnell Map was their sole reference in marking the boundary, the commissioners must use the grid coordinates as given on the map. Bartlett countered that since the coordinates were in error, the map should be used for position purposes only, and that the land boundary should be surveyed along a line 8 miles north of Juarez.

The commissioners compromised by trading latitude for longitude. Conde would get the New Mexico boundary 42 miles above Juarez at latitude 32 deg., 22 min., and Bartlett would get the line extended 175.28 miles, or 3 deg. of longitude, west into what is now Arizona. In order to bind both countries legally to the compromise, it was necessary for the commissioner and surveyor of each country to sign the agreement. Conde, Salazar, and Bartlett signed immediately, but Gray was back in Washington ill with smallpox. Bartlett wanted to effect the compromise without delay, and had his interim surveyor Lieutenant Whipple sign for Gray; Whipple signed under protest.

By April, 1851 the joint commission was busily running the survey west from a point on the River above what is now Las Cruces, New Mexico. Bartlett was a very happy man. He had effected a compromise which insured the United States possession of the rich Santa Rita copper deposits. Surely his superiors in Washington would not forget his deeds. Surely he would be rewarded.

Unfortunately, Bartlett did not realize he had given away the only possible route for a southern transcontinental railroad, the route Major Emory had seen and recommended from earlier surveys. Also, Gray returned from Washington in July, 1851 and invalidated the Bartlett-Conde compromise by not acknowledging Whipple's signature. Gray argued that errors in the grid on Disturnell's map should not affect the boundary, and that the land boundary should run west from the Rio Grande a few miles above Juarez, as shown on the treaty map (latitude 31 deg., 52 min.). Bartlett, who had already yielded in a compromise with Conde, had no choice but to refuse recognition of Gray's proposed line. The survey was interrupted once again (Douglas, 1930: 38).

Bartlett was about to face another succession of complications. Democrats in Washington pressed the administration to secure the southern railroad route. Bartlett knew the compromise line would have to be moved south, or be done away with entirely. Then, in December, 1851, Commissioner Conde died in Sonora. The United States Commissioner in effect abdicated by leaving Gray and his men on the Gila River, but taking with him most of the commission's finances. What followed was a one year junket by Bartlett to Acapulco, Mazatlan, San Diego, California, and eventually back to El Paso (James, 1970).

During Bartlett's absence, Gray was replaced on the commission by Major Emory. Upon reaching the United States commission at El Paso, Emory found that:

. . . with the exception of one or two, none were fitted for the service on which they were engaged; most of them ignorant of the first principles of surveying, and embroiled in feuds with each other . . . the commissioner . . . or . . . the scientific corps (Emory, 1857: 10-11).

He also received orders from the Secretary of the Interior to sign the original Bartlett-Conde compromise and effect the survey, apparently because of the embarrassment suffered by the administration in not being able to establish the boundary. Emory knew the compromise would not provide the railroad route. More importantly, he was also the first to realize that the original line shown on the Disturnell Map would not have provided the railroad route. Very wisely, Emory signed the compromise with the notation that he was a witness only.

Commissioner Emory (Unofficial)

Emory apparently was held in high esteem both by Whigs and by Democrats, for, according to his personal account, he had been offered the original commissionership by President Polk. The offer was contingent on his resignation from the military, which he declined (Emory, 1857: 1). Now, several years later and in the absence of Bartlett, he provided the leadership that would eventually fix the boundary.

During 1852, Emory's crews surveyed the lower Rio Grande, setting up observation posts at Frontera, San Elizario, and Eagle Pass. Repeated attempts at securing promised funds from either Washington or Bartlett proved futile. Even those drafts received were not honored. Of the funds previously expended by Bartlett, Emory found less than 20 percent appropriated for survey-related work. At the same time, Expansionists in Congress saddled additional survey funds until the Bartlett-Conde Line was repudiated. Some of Emory's men became very insubordinate after they had:

... not received any pay for eighteen months, and the commissioner [Bartlett] was at the moment, with an equipage and corps of attendants, visiting the States of Chihuahua and Sonora, and the Geysers of California — places sufficiently distant from the line (Emory, 1857: 11).

Bartlett returned from Mexico and rejoined the commission at Eagle Pass in December, 1852. Shortly thereafter he resigned his commission and returned to New England. Although his appointment had been a catastrophe for the United States commission, Bartlett took excellent notes of his journeys through Mexico and matched his text with vivid plates. His *Personal Narrative* has been a priceless source for historians and geographers of the southwest (Bartlett, 1854).

Commissioner Campbell

After Bartlett's resignation, the boundary commission formally disbanded at Eagle Pass. Emory left his crews and returned to Washington to obtain funds necessary to finish his survey. Funds were supplied, and Emory returned to the River with the new commissioner, Robert Campbell. Emory resumed the survey in March, 1853 and directed the crews below Eagle Pass; by December, 1853, the boundary was fixed from the Gulf to El Paso.

Gadsden Purchase

At the same time that Emory resumed the River survey, March, 1853, Franklin Pierce took office as President. A Democrat, Pierce appointed James Gadsden as Minister to Mexico and gave him explicit orders to buy the disputed tract of land extending west from the Mesilla Valley, and any additional land that might be required for the railroad.

Gadsden made several offers to Mexico. At a maximum, he wanted Lower California, northern Sonora, Chihuahua, and Coahuila for 50 million dollars. This acquisition would have placed the boundary across the rugged Sierra Madre and would have ended existing survey problems. At a minimum, he wanted the boundary at the 32nd parallel, or just enough area for the railroad. Mexico would get 15 million dollars. Along with his offers, the Minister included a threat of occupation if Mexico refused to sell. Mexico, in financial straits, capitulated and signed a treaty in December, 1853 that elaborated on Gadsden's minimum offer of 15 million dollars (Utley, 1964: 18-20).

Gadsden returned to Washington and saw sectional interests in the Senate vote down ratification of the treaty. The treaty was amended and ratified in April, 1854. In the final Gadsden Purchase, Mexico received only 10 million dollars and the United States got the irregular boundary we have today (10 Stat. 1031). Significantly, the boundary leaves the River in El Paso, at 31 deg., 47 min. north latitude, or well south of the lines of both the Bartlett-Conde compromise and the Disturnell Map (Utley, 1964: 23-25) (Fig. III-2).

Commissioner Emory (Official)

Shortly after the Senate's ratification, Pierce appointed Emory commissioner, surveyor, and chief astronomer. The Mexican commission was headed by Salazar, Conde's successor and Emory's old friend. Together the commissioners completed the survey without incident. The boundary was proclaimed in October, 1855, seven years after Guadalupe Hidalgo (Utley, 1964: 40-48).

Figure III-2. *View looking east at the junction of the fluvial and land segments of the international boundary. Monument Number 1 in foreground is surrounded by park area that was dedicated in December, 1972. To the left is the American Dam that diverts water into the Franklin Canal system of El Paso. The Franklin Mountains and El Paso appear in the far left horizon, partially obliterated from view by the slag pile of a large copper smelter.* (Photo by the author.)

IV

International Law and the Restless River 1855-1889

ⱳ Unlike nation states, which govern themselves internally through legislative, judicial, and executive bodies, the world has no organization fully empowered to write laws, enforce laws, and review laws. Instead, specific international law is based on agreement among nations, effected by the treaties and conventions to which countries choose to bind themselves. Because each country is a partner to treaties not shared by all other nations, it follows that the composition of international law as envisioned by any one country must be unique.

Problems between countries often arise which are either not specifically governed by existing treaties, or lead to differences in treaty interpretation. Such problems are usually resolved by (1) Compromise within the existing framework of treaties; (2) Signing a new treaty; (3) Submitting the issues to international and special courts. If the latter route is chosen, the international and special courts must resort to precedents established in the evolution of treaties among other nations and to the decisions and awards of the other courts. Here, international law becomes a very heterogeneous composite of past relationships among countries, i.e., law is replaced by precedents, customs, and mores. According to Hackworth:

International law consists of a body of rules governing the relations between states. It is a system of jurisprudence which, for the most part, has evolved out of the experiences and the necessities of situations that have arisen from time to time. It has developed with the progress of civilization and with the increasing realization by nations that their relations *inter se,* if not their existence, must be governed by and depend upon rules of law fairly certain and generally reasonable. Customary, as distinguished from conventional, international law is based upon the common consent of nations extending over a period of time of sufficient duration to cause it to become crystallized into a rule of conduct. When doubt arises as to the existence or nonexistence of a rule of international law, or as to the application of a rule to a given situation, resort is usually had to such sources as pertinent treaties, pronouncements of foreign offices, statements by writers, and decisions of international tribunals and those of prize courts and other domestic courts purporting to be expressive of the law of nations (Hackworth, 1940: 1).

Rivers as Boundaries

Only in the past few hundred years have rivers become important as international boundaries. Previously they had been a no-man's-land or natural barrier that served to keep various ethnic groups segregated. A growing sedentary population, increased commerce and navigation, and colonialism all demanded guidelines and regulations that would define and protect riparian rights of countries adjacent to international streams (Swift, 1969: 186). The ancients practiced the principle of co-dominion, whereby a stream's entire width would be held in common by neighboring countries. Later, Vattel and Grotius suggested equality of division, or using the middle of a river as boundary. This idea proved very practical on non-navigable streams where division of area was of primary consideration (Hackworth, 1940: 573).

Rivers throughout geologic time have proved to be short-lived, transient phenomena. Countless numbers of streams have become obliterated by channel filling, stream piracy, continental glaciation, encroachment of the seas, climatic change, etc. Even within the life of man, a river's course is not likely to be permanent unless it is contained in unerodible walls and does not have the capacity to completely clog its channel with alluvium. River volume shrinks and swells at the mercy of climate, and most rivers must make accompanying adjustments in their channel geometry. They erode, deposit, meander, and occasionally abandon their former courses in periods of extreme flood. For this reason it is fortunate that many areas of the world avoid rivers as international boundaries. Most boundaries in Europe follow drainage divides, especially along mountain crests. The Pyrenees between Spain and France and the Alps between Austria and Italy are prime examples. These boundaries tend to be fairly permanent and remote, and conflicts over their exact position are few. According to Gregory:

... natural boundaries through all the ages have proved the most success-ful. They have the advantage of being readily demarcated; they are inex-pensive and immovable; they endure under all conditions of climate . . . (Gregory, 1937: 11).

The reference here must be toward mountain divides, although it can be questioned how readily the backbone of rugged uplands can be demarcated. Also, the Rio Grande, a natural fluvial boundary, has been both mobile and expensive. Hyde concluded that:

... the United States of America has had at least eight times as much trou-ble with water boundaries as with mountain boundaries. But this is an understatement of the situation, for . . . the Rio Bravo del Norte or Rio Grande, has already caused trouble at some 89 localities. It caused this trouble in a period of only 65 years. And it is absolutely certain that it will cause similar trouble and expense at hundreds of other localities in years to come (Hyde, 1947: 443).

International Law of River Boundaries

International boundary rivers tend to be governed by one of two sets of law, depending upon whether or not the rivers are navigable. Unfortunately, there is no single test of navigability. According to Moore, a navigable stream must be able to transport goods essential to trade or agriculture during periods of normal flow. He concludes that the Rio Grande is a non-navigable stream in its New Mexico reach (Moore, 1906: 621-22). This is an understatement. Even prior to reservoir building, the Rio Grande probably was not a navigable stream anywhere along its course, except in its extreme downstream reach near Brownsville. Elsewhere the River is either broad and shal-low, or constricted by canyons with rapids and falls. Yet it is not un-common in the El Paso-Juarez Valley to hear tales of ocean-going vessels that supposedly docked and traded goods with the local popu-lace. Anyone familiar with the course of the Rio Grande between the Gulf of Mexico and El Paso will recognize the impossibility of such a feat.

It seems likely that the journal entries of Spanish explorers who ascended the lower Rio Grande have been responsible for labeling the River as navigable. A question arises as to how much of a stream must be navigable in order to have the entire stream labeled as such. International law apparently does not recognize a given stream as being both navigable and non-navigable. Therefore, if an international court determines that a boundary river is navigable in one reach, but not in another, the set of laws related to navigable streams will apply to the entire river, and the boundary will be delineated as though the entire river were navigable.

Non-navigable international rivers generally have their boundary line placed in the middle of the channel; where the stream is multi-channeled, the line is everywhere midway between the outermost channels. In the latter case, it is common to find the boundary line traversing islands which occupy a portion of the mid-line. Thus the boundary might have both fluvial and land segments, and some islands will be shared by neighbors (Sahovic and Bishop, 1968: 320).

This principle of equality of division as advanced by Grotius and Vattel seldom applies to navigable international streams. Instead, it is there replaced by the principle of thalweg. Thalweg is derived from German, and translated literally means "valley way," "down way," or "down valley" (Swift, 1969: 186 and Moore, 1968: 207). The various disciplines which have adopted the term have given thalweg very special meanings. Geologists, for example, define thalweg as a line that joins the lowest points of a valley or the deepest points of a river channel (American Geological Institute, 1960: 296). If such a trace is shown in cross-section, it is referred to as a longitudinal or valley profile, and generally extends concave upward from the mouth to the head of either a valley or stream (Monkhouse, 1970: 347). When drawn on a map to denote the line of maximum depth of a river, the geologists' thalweg forms a very irregular and sinuous trace (Gilluly, et al., 1968: 231).

In international law, thalweg refers to that trace of channel which in navigable streams is best suited for water commerce (navigation). In the establishment of boundaries based on the principle of thalweg, it has been customary to mark the middle of the thalweg channel as the boundary, rather than the absolute thalweg itself. This is done because the thalweg trace is very irregular, even in relatively straight channels, and would produce the longest possible fluvial boundary and the most difficult survey. In addition, the absolute thalweg is quite mobile, especially in alluvial streams like the Rio Grande. The thalweg channel also may in rare instances not necessarily be the deepest channel, for the current might be too swift for navigation. Conversely, very wide channels are often too shallow to permit navigation (Hyde, 1947: 445). Finally, a thalweg boundary has the distinct advantage of being entirely fluvial, i.e., river islands and bars must lie entirely within the domain of a single country (Gould, 1957: 362).

In order to insure equal navigation rights to adjacent riverine states, the principle of thalweg replaced equality of division in Europe by the end of the eighteenth century. The thalweg principle, as defined and proclaimed at the Congress of Rastadt in 1797, was incorporated into the 1801 Treaty of Luneville, the first treaty to mention the principle by name. In North America the principle, but not the term, was used as early as 1842 in the Webster-Ashburton Treaty that defined the boundary along the St. John River. The first mention of the term thalweg in a United States treaty can be traced to a 1908 convention with Canada in which the United States-Canadian boundary along the St. Croix River was established.

In many cases, it has been customary in the United States to invoke the thalweg principle when deciding boundary suits between states separated by a navigable river, even if the boundaries were originally determined by treaties that preceded the rise of the thalweg principle in North America. Cases involving the fluvial boundaries between Iowa and Illinois, Louisiana and Mississippi, Minnesota and Wisconsin, and Delaware and New Jersey are examples where the United States Supreme Court has applied the thalweg principle retroactively. On the other hand, the Hague Court in 1916 ruled that the fluvial boundary between Norway and Sweden could not be demarcated by thalweg because the original boundary treaty between the two countries in 1658 preceded the rise of the thalweg principle (Hackworth, 1940: 573-75). No evidence has been found to suggest that the thalweg principle has ever been used retroactively on international boundaries described before the middle of the eighteenth century.

Some Aspects of River Morphology

The ability of a stream to maintain its plan position depends on several factors, including the amount and variability of discharge conveyed through the channel, composition of bed and bank material, gradient or slope, and the amount and types of vegetation. A shift in the position of a stream is unlikely where the channel is contained by deep valleys or canyons and where bedrock valley walls descend directly to the water's edge. At the other extreme, rivers that flow across broad alluvial floodplains are likely to adjust fairly rapidly to high discharges at a given cross-section by flowing faster (increasing velocity), scouring the bed (deepening), cutting laterally (widening), flooding, and occasionally abandoning existing channels in favor of new ones.

In humid areas of the world, chemical weathering of certain minerals, especially the silicates, produces very stable end products called clays. These clays, when added to the soil or the alluvium of floodplains, increase the cohesiveness or shear strength of the unconsolidated bank material by forming a fine-textured matrix in which larger particles of silt, sand, and gravel are held. Bank cohesiveness is also directly related to vegetation density, which in turn is related to climate. This cohesiveness leads to increased thresholds of erosion and greater bank stability along some floodplains and even allows rivers to build and maintain meanders. Therefore, at or near bankfull discharge, these same rivers adjust most in velocity and depth, and least in width. Also, it is not uncommon after flood discharges to find where the overbank discharge cut through the base of a floodplain meander and abandoned a segment of the old channel. This latter case indicates that the relatively cohesive bank material would not allow the stream to adjust its width rapidly enough to compensate for the increased discharge.

The production of clays in a given area is enhanced by the supply of heat, moisture, and organic material, the latter two combining in solution to react with mineral matter. Therefore, it is understandable that the ultimate in chemical weathering and clay production should be found in the densely forested tropics. Moderate amounts of clay are produced in the humid mid-latitudes, whereas little is produced in polar and subhumid regions, the former lacking excess heat, the latter being deficient in rainfall. All this should not suggest that clays are entirely absent from the drier parts of the world. Along the upper Rio Grande, for example, surface erosion locally uncovers and transports into the River system a moderate abundance of clay minerals. These clays developed under more humid conditions several thousand years ago and were subsequently buried by younger soils. In addition, fine airborne dust also settles on the basin and is incorporated into the soils, banks, and floodplains.

In subhumid regions of the world, it is typical to find alluvial or floodplain rivers that do not meander as much as their humid area counterparts. This difference in meandering tendency can be attributed in part to the relatively slow rates of chemical weathering, the usual paucity of clay fractions in soils and alluvium, and the absence of dense vegetation cover in the subhumid zones. Differences in flow regimes also account for the difference in bank stability between humid and subhumid rivers. It is a general rule of thumb that, as total rainfall decreases, reliability of rainfall also decreases. In subhumid areas, the seemingly low annual rainfall is often concentrated in a few convective storms, which, when combined with the sparse vegetation cover, lead to flash flooding. On the other hand, while streams in humid regions tend to be perennial, those in subhumid regions are often dry at least part of the year. It follows then, that the greater the variability in flow regime, the lesser the chance for effective vegetation to take hold and anchor bank materials.

Without the necessary binding agents to stabilize river banks, and the highly variable flow regimes, it is not surprising that during high discharge most alluvial rivers in subhumid zones adjust their width more rapidly than do alluvial streams of humid areas. Therefore, the width to depth ratios of rivers in subhumid zones are substantially higher than those for humid areas (Schumm, 1960: 17-30). As a consequence, it is more difficult to flood along many rivers in subhumid regions owing to the tremendous capacity of the channel to widen. These circumstances also lessen the possibility of meander development and the abandonment of meander loops during peak discharges, but do contribute to internal braiding and innumerable shifts in the thalweg channel. The same can be said for many rivers in higher latitudes where flow regimes are related to outwash from ablating valley glaciers. In winter their source of water is frozen, whereas in late spring and early summer meltwaters gush across the alluvial outwash plains in intensely-braided systems.

It should be evident from the section on fluvial boundaries that the body of international law dealing with river boundaries was developed from precedents established in western Europe and the eastern United States, two major humid regions of the world. Likewise, that portion of international law that maintains or reestablishes fluvial boundaries in response to changes in channel position, was also developed in humid areas. Therefore, we have in international law today a set of procedures dealing with fluvial boundaries which has in some cases, been forced upon arid zone rivers. It is understandable that these rivers in the subhumid parts of the world cannot fully comply with the rules and regulations imposed by treaty makers and jurists.

Channel Changes and International Law

The extremes in channel changes along alluvial rivers are those associated with minimum and maximum discharges. During low flow, the channel might aggrade or deposit alluvium against both banks. During moderate flows, it might scour at one point and fill at another. This dual activity is common along meandering streams where water velocity increases from the inside to the outside of a meander bend, and where deposition on the inside bend is accompanied by erosion or scour on the outside bend. The net effect is a slow lateral migration of the meander and its thalweg. During peak discharges, shortening of the river by meander cutoffs will completely abandon segments of the former channel and thalweg.

The process of channel change that occurs within existing river banks is recognized as accretion or alluvion in international law. It is the day to day process of slowly removing soil particles from one bank and depositing soil particles against another. When this occurs, the fluvial boundary migrates horizontally with the channel and thalweg. The implication here is that the channel changes are gradual enough to be imperceptible at a given point in time (Hyde, 1947: 355). According to Oppenheim:

Accretion is the name for the increase of land through new formations. And it is the customary rule of the Law of Nations that enlargement of territory if created through new formations, takes place *ipso facto,* by accretion, without the state concerned taking any special step for the purpose of extending its sovereignty. Accretion must therefore be considered as a mode of acquiring territory (Oppenheim, 1928, II: 299-300).

In the case of islands where the channel is forced to bifurcate, it is possible through accretion to clog the main channel and force the thalweg to shift to the opposite side of the island. Numerous European precedents suggest that when this occurs, the former sovereign and owner retain title to the island, but the new sovereign gains supreme control over the island and exercises its rights of law, taxation, etc. (Hyde, 1947: 449).

The process by which a river suddenly abandons its previous course during peak discharges in favor of a new one is termed avulsion. When this occurs, the boundary remains in the old channel, even if the old channel should become wholly dry. A qualification for avulsion is that it be perceptible at a given point in time. Cutoffs of meanders on floodplains during flood stage are probably the best examples of avulsion. According to one author, perceptible or rapid erosion within an existing channel also constitutes avulsion, but most writers restrict the term to channel abandonment only.

International law in general seems to be imbued with the idea that erosion and accretion are slow and gradual processes, whereas avulsion is accomplished by sudden, violent means (Utley, 1964: 84). There are no provisions for either rapid and violent erosion, or for gradual avulsion. The sliding and slumping of undercut river banks are good examples of perceptible, rapid, and violent erosion. These processes are especially common along arid zone rivers that have non-cohesive banks. In the same sense, many goosenecks of meanders are cut through by stream sapping at the narrows of the bend, a process which can be very slow and gradual. Also, it is possible to have accretion on one bank and avulsion on the other if the processes are defined in terms of perceptibility. In one such case, *Nebraska vs. Iowa*, the United States Supreme Court ruled that where both processes are operating, the rule of accretion applies, and the boundary shifts with the channel (Hyde, 1947: 447).

Restless River 1855-1884

At the time of the original Emory-Salazar surveys, the lower Rio Grande Valley was very sparsely populated, and the precise location of the fluvial boundary was of little concern. Interest in its location increased rapidly as subsequent agricultural, industrial, and mining centers became established along the River. As early as 1856, J. W. Magoffin, a Texas citizen, wrote Commissioner Emory about a threatened avulsive change in the River's course. What effect would such a change have on Emory's original survey? The Commissioner promptly forwarded Magoffin's letter to Washington for an official reply. The opinion rendered by United States Attorney General Caleb Cushing traced the history of fluvial boundaries, including the principle of thalweg. His opinion was to become the official United States position regarding fluvial boundaries.

The respective territories of the United States and of the Mexican Republic are arcifinious; that is to say, territories separated not only by a mathematical line, but by natural objects of indeterminate natural extension which of themselves serve to *keep off* the public enemy.

. . .

When a river is the dividing limit of arcifinious territories, the natural changes to which it is liable, or which its action may produce in the face of the country, give rise to various questions. . . .

. . .

With such conditions, whatever changes happen to either bank of the river by accretion on the one, or degradation on the other, that is, by the gradual, as it were, insensible accession or obstruction of mere particles, the river as it runs continues to be the boundary.

. . .

The general aspect of things remains unchanged.

. . .

But on the other hand, if, deserting its original bed, the river forces for it-self a new channel in another direction, then the nation, through whose territory the river thus breaks its way, suffers injury by the loss of territory greater than the benefit of retaining the natural river boundary, and that boundary remains in the middle of the deserted river bed (Cushing, 1856: 175).

Cushing's opinion is significant in that it solidifies the position in international law that river changes are either gradual accretion or sudden avulsion. There is no recognition of intermediate processes in Cushing's opinion. Also, he obviously assumed that unless treaties specified otherwise, river boundaries were not fixed lines. Such was his view of the Rio Grande despite the fact that he paraphrased the 1848 Treaty as follows:

The treaty further provides that Commissioners appointed by the two governments shall survey and work out upon the land the stipulated line, which, as agreed upon and established by them, shall in all time be faith-fully respected, without any variation therein, unless by express and full consent of both republics (Cushing, 1856: 175).

During the decade following Cushing's opinion, the lower Rio Grande was severely flooded several times. Meanders were aban-doned avulsively; erosion and accretion rates were both imperceptible and rapid. Farther upstream, in the Mesilla Valley north of El Paso, flood discharges in the 1860's estimated at between 25,000 and 50,000 c.f.s. ravaged an area whose natural channel capacity was estimated to be only 10,000 c.f.s. (Gile, et al., 1970: 135). When the floods sub-sided, the active channel was displaced nearly one mile westward to where the flood waters had scoured an old Indian irrigation canal. Unfortunately, there are no discharge records for the Rio Grande at El Paso prior to 1889 by means of which one might be able to associ-ate types and rates of channel change with specific discharges. How-ever, there is some eyewitness evidence that, even during record floods along the River, there were areas in which the water remained confined to the active channel where banks were especially friable and easily eroded. Some of this evidence is offered in the chapter on Chamizal.

In 1867, the Mexican Government inquired of Secretary of State

Seward concerning the effect on the boundary of channel changes that occurred in the preceding few years. Seward simply restated the United States' position by forwarding a copy of Cushing's 1856 opinion. The Mexican Minister replied that:

I have read that opinion with interest, and it has appeared to me that the principles enunciated therein are equitable and founded on the teachings of the most accredited expositors of international law.

. . .

It pertains to the government of Mexico to express its conformity to or dissent from these principles . . . I hesitate not to adopt them, meanwhile as reasonable and equitable (Romero to Seward, 1867 in Chamizal, U.S. *Appendix*, 1911: 565-66).

There is no evidence that the Mexican Government sanctioned or rejected Romero's acceptance. Nevertheless, Romero's acceptance strongly suggests that at least some Mexican officials as early as 1867 regarded the boundary as mobile.

In 1871 Mexico again confronted the United States with the question of channel and boundary change. She charged that the Wharf Company of Brownsville violated the 1848 Treaty by building dikes and impeding navigation. Further, she blamed the rising water levels behind the dikes for increasing accretion on the United States bank at the expense of erosion on the Mexican bank. The United States Consul at Matamoros, T. F. Wilson, investigated the complaint and reported that it was in fact the Mexican bank which was receiving deposits, whereas the United States bank was being eroded. Also, he concluded that all changes had been effected by natural causes, and that these changes were prevalent elsewhere along the Rio Grande. In addition:

The local authorities of both countries collect taxes and exercise jurisdiction . . . where these changes have taken place, apparently in conformity with the principle of law enunciated in the opinion of Attorney General Cushing, . . . (Wilson to Hunter, 1871, in Chamizal, U.S. *Appendix*, 1911: 574-76).

Mexico apparently accepted Wilson's findings, for no objections or official protests were filed. Yet, there is some evidence that Mexico was essentially adhering to a fixed-line theory already in the 1870's, one based on the text of the 1848 Treaty, and one which was wholly incompatible with Cushing's opinion.

It should be borne in mind that when marking the boundary, the points through which it should pass were fixed astronomically, which indicates the wish of both Nations that there never should be any increase of territory.

It is clear that the boundaries which are definitely established when the treaty was celebrated, constituted mathematical lines to be thenceforth considered as invariable; and that no provision was made for the event not then foreseen, that the rivers, suddenly changing their course, should penetrate into either of the two territories, dismembering them in such a way as to render the boundaries indefinite and imaginary, with irreparable detriment to one of the two Nations, whose territorial rights would be at the mercy of an unexpected change in the currents of the river (Lafragua to Mariscal, 1874, in Chamizal, U.S. *Argument*, 1911: 44-45).

In 1875 Mexico offered the United States a plan which was not agreed upon immediately, but which became the basis of the Treaty of 1884. The plan contained provisions for determining the boundary after channel changes occurred and complied with accepted international law. Thus, it also recognized fluvial boundaries as variable lines (Timm, 1941: 153-54).

When Emory surveyed the lower Rio Grande near Roma, Texas in 1853, he discovered that the River contained three channels and two islands. Upon further investigation, he concluded that the narrowest, but deepest (thalweg), channel lay against the Mexican shore, and that the islands were in the jurisdiction of the United States. In subsequent decades the center channel filled through gradual accretion, and the thalweg shifted to the northernmost channel against the United States bank (Gregory, 1937: 167). The large composite island, known as Morteritos, was rightfully claimed in 1884 by the Mexican Government in accordance with the principle of thalweg and the rules of change through accretion and avulsion. Cushing's opinion notwithstanding, the United States rejected the claim and invoked its own fixed-line theory. Because the United States joined Mexico in espousing an invariable boundary, Mexico withdrew her claim to the island. The Mexican Minister wrote that:

It is very satisfactory to me to see that in this important point there is a uniformity of views and principles between our two governments (Romero to Frelinghuysen, 1884, in Chamizal, U.S. *Appendix*, 1911: 669).

Treaty of 1884

Shortly after the settlement of Morteritos, Secretary of State Frelinghuysen and Mexican Minister Romero signed a convention which conformed to Cushing's 1856 opinion of a variable boundary line. The convention was essentially a modification of the plan submitted by Mexico in 1875. According to Articles 1 and 2 of the Treaty of 1884:

> The dividing line shall forever be that described in the aforesaid treaty and follow the center of the normal channel of the rivers named, notwithstanding any alterations in the banks or in the course of those rivers, provided that such alterations be effected by natural causes through the slow and gradual erosion and deposition of alluvium and not by the abandonment of an existing river bed and the opening of a new one.
>
> Any other change, wrought by the force of the current, whether by the cutting of a new bed, or when there is more than one channel by the deepening of another channel than that which marked the boundary at the time of the survey made under the aforesaid treaty, shall produce no change in the dividing line as fixed . . . in 1852; but the line then fixed shall continue to follow the middle of the original channel bed . . . (24 Stat. 1011).

While these provisions in general conform to international law, they are also ambiguous. Accretion is restricted to a rate of "slow and gradual" with no quantitative statement of its limits. Avulsive changes that produce no change in the boundary include both channel abandonment and the deepening of one channel at the expense of another. Interestingly, there is no mention of the rate at which these occur. Since accretion is limited to "slow and gradual," avulsive changes might imply sudden, violent processes. Another interpretation is that they could occur through processes ranging from very slow to very sudden. What happens in the case of rapid erosion? One interpretation might be that since it is excluded under accretion, it must be a type of avulsion. Another interpretation is that since it is not specifically mentioned, it is not governed by the treaty, and hence it is neither accretion nor avulsion.

If a thalweg shifts from one channel to another where a river has multiple channels, international law usually dictates an accompanying shift in the boundary if the process involved was accretion. There-fore, the Morteritos Island settlement in favor of the United States circumvented accepted international law, as does the provision in the Treaty of 1884 that deals with multiple channels.

The treaty also has provisions for protecting the rights of property owners in areas of boundary shifts, as well as that of navigation. In the latter case:

... no one seriously intended to navigate the Rio Grande or the Colorado, but the legal fiction was maintained for many years and obstructed for a time the great dam-building programs of the 20th century (Utley, 1964: 88).

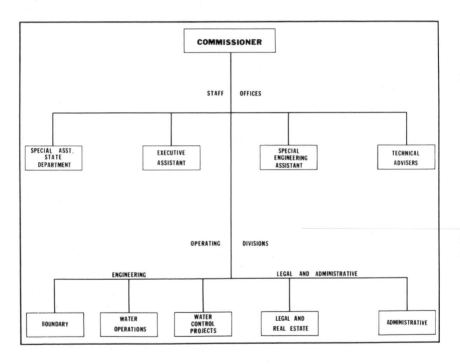

FIGURE V-1. *Structure of the United States Section, International Boundary and Water Commission.*

V

ESTABLISHING THE INTERNATIONAL
BOUNDARY COMMISSION

ꙮ Prior to the Treaty of 1884, the United States and Mexico had authorized by treaty three temporal joint commissions charged with either an original survey or the remarking of the boundary. The authorization came from the Treaties of 1848, 1853, and 1882. With the advent of the Treaty of 1884 came the question of who would administer its stipulations. Another boundary commission was imminent, and events in the El Paso-Juarez Valley prompted its formation.

Since the original Emory-Salazar survey of the early 1850's, the Rio Grande had by the middle 1880's shifted far to the south between Juarez and El Paso. Accordingly, several hundred acres of land in the upper El Paso-Juarez Valley were eroded from the Mexican shore while a similar amount had been added to south El Paso. In order to curb further encroachment of the River, Juarez officials authorized the construction of several wing dams on the Mexican bank. These wing dams were attached to the Mexican shore and extended obliquely downstream toward the center of the channel in an effort to force the current away from the Mexican bank. They were constructed of mattressed layers of brush tied in bundles called *fascines*. Each layer was floated into position and sunk by a load of rock dumped on its surface. Succeeding layers were built and attached in a similar manner. By the end of 1888, five dams ranging in length from 325 to 500 feet and projecting into the channel between 60 and 250 feet were completed. Depending on water depth, river width, and current, their angle with the Mexican shore varied between 13 and 50 degrees.

The City of El Paso complained to the United States State Department that the change in current and subsequent artificially-induced erosion of the American bank violated existing treaties. Also, the city warned that a major Mexican dam was proposed that would extend completely across the Rio Grande and would have one terminus on the Texas shore. The State Department sent a Major Ernst to investigate the complaint, to check on the nature of channel movement, and to report on the effect that future Mexican proposals would have on the River's position. Prior to Ernst's arrival in El Paso, the Mexican Government replied that the proposed dam was merely another in the series of wing dams and would not extend more than a fraction of the way across the active channel. Also, a serious disagreement over the boundary between El Paso and Juarez was imminent when the Mexican Government tried to dismiss the problem of the proposed dam by stating that:

It is not true that the part of the River in which the works are conducted is the boundary line, that line lying a great distance to the north, and not having yet been changed, by the two Governments (Mariscal to Whitehouse, 1888, in Chamizal, U.S. *Appendix*, 1911: 733).

This interpretation of the boundary in 1888 by Mexico was based on the text of the 1848 Treaty and obviously did not consider the 1884 Treaty to be retroactive.

Major Ernst's report to the Secretary of State indicated that one of the proposed wing dams would cross midchannel and in fact be in the State of Texas, according to the text of the 1884 Treaty. Ernst also forwarded a report by the Mexican engineer Garfias that reinforced the Mexican position that the active channel was wholly Mexican (Ernst to Bayard, 1888, in Chamizal, U.S. *Appendix*, 1911: 758-81). This stalemate over the location of the boundary, plus the disagreement over the construction of a sewer drain pipe and the construction of diversion works by independent irrigators, demanded solution and regulation by another joint boundary commission. In 1889, a treaty was signed that established the International Boundary Commission, whose tenure was to expire in 1894. Yearly extensions of the treaty beyond 1894 led to a permanent Commission in 1900.

The basic function of the new Commission was to hear cases on channel changes along the Rio Grande, to decide whether such changes were due to avulsion or erosion and accretion, then to apply the Treaty of 1884 to determine if the tract in dispute was Mexican or United States territory. According to Article 1 of the Treaty of 1889:

All differences or questions that may arise on that portion of the frontier . . . where the . . . Rivers form the boundary line, whether such differences or questions grow out of alterations or changes in the bed . . . or of works that may be constructed in said rivers . . . shall be submitted for examination and decision to an International Boundary Commission, which shall have exclusive jurisdiction in the case of said differences or questions (26 *Stat.* 1512).

In addition, the treaty provided for the basic membership of the Commission, with commissioners to be appointed by their respective president (Fig. V-1). Very importantly, the Commission was to be situated on the boundary; the sister cities of El Paso, Texas and Ciudad Juarez, Chihuahua were chosen. Powers to summon witnesses and to call for local documents and papers were also provided.

The Early Commission

The Commission was not formally organized until 1894, nearly five years after the Treaty of 1889 was signed. President Cleveland appointed a military man, Colonel Anson Mills, as United States Commissioner. During the first few years of the Commission, Mills and the Mexican Commissioner Osorno concentrated their efforts on resolving the numerous banco cases (Chapter VI). Bancos are meander cutoffs formed when the neck of a river bend is severed from the mainland. When this occurs, parcels of land become detached from one sovereign and attached to the other, although the former sovereign retains title according to international law and the Treaty of 1884, i.e., the boundary remains in the old dry channel.

Several immediate problems confronted the commissioners. First, where the River was especially active in shifting its course, multiple bancos could be found adjacent to a modern river bend, and the determination of whether or not each had formed avulsively, or by gradual erosion, was nearly impossible. Second, where avulsion had occurred and the channel and boundary became dry, cultivation had often obliterated the old channel, and hence the boundary could not be marked (Utley, 1964: 91-92). The commissioners must also have recognized that if portions of the boundary were allowed to become dry, the River would contain an infinite number of reaches, some wholly Mexican, some wholly United States, and yet others international.

As a solution, both commissioners recommended to their governments that bancos become territory of the nation to which they are attached, although individual property rights to banco lands should not be impaired (Mills, 1921: 279). Consequently, the boundary would remain fluvial. A new treaty was necessary to effect these recommendations, but was not signed until 1905 (Chapter VI).

The Modern Commission

Two important changes in the Commission have occurred since its inception in 1894. A 1944 Treaty dealing with the use of international waters changed the Commission's name to the International Boundary and Water Commission. The same treaty provided that commissioners must be engineers.

The modern Commission maintains field offices along the international boundary in addition to its headquarters in El Paso and Juarez. Each field office is assigned a reach of the River along which to observe actual and potential channel changes induced by natural or artificial causes. Heads of field offices exchange information, hold joint inspections, and undertake minor corrective measures.

Major corrective measures are undertaken by the Commission after both commissioners agree that a problem submitted to them is in fact international. International problems usually arise when the two countries need benefits that require joint works on the boundary and in the territory of the two countries; when one country needs a benefit that requires construction works in the other; or when one country is, or could be, damaged by situations in the other.

Sometimes solutions are unilateral, especially in problems arising from man-made situations. As an example, sewage emitted from Tijuana once reached the United States beaches on the Pacific Coast, while sewage from Brownsville was discharged to the Rio Grande and affected both countries. Each country undertook independent sewage treatment measures to correct the problems. Other unilateral solutions are generally in the area of flood control or riprap protection along banks. Even when unilateral solutions are sought, however, the commissioners generally review one another's plans.

Bilateral solutions are probably the most common and important measures undertaken. Large-scale flood control projects, diversion dams, channel rectification, and some sewage treatment plants are joint ventures. Douglas, Arizona and Agua Prieta, Sonora shared sewage treatment facilities, and the two Nogaleses have joint facilities.

In 1941, Nogales, Sonora suppressed her plans for a city sewer system because the terrain generally sloped northward toward Nogales, Arizona. An obvious solution was to treat Mexican sewage in Arizona. By 1951, a Mexican outfall line was connected to the Arizona system at the international boundary. From there the sewage was pumped to a treatment plant whose effluent was used to irrigate Arizona cropland. The project cost each section of the Commission approximately a quarter million dollars (I.B.W.C. *Report*, 1954: 23-24). This project was jointly improved in 1971 at a total cost of 30 million dollars.

Requests for funding the United States Section are sent to the executive branch where, if approved, they are forwarded to Congress as part of the State Department's appropriation requests. The Mexican Commissioner submits solutions to his Ministry of Foreign Relations, which solicits construction from the appropriate Mexican Departments. The rapidity with which solutions are carried out is enhanced by the fact that personnel of both Sections can work free of immigration and custom control in each other's territory in the performance of joint works (Herrera and Friedkin, 1967: 2-5).

The scale of operation of the United States Section is reflected in the size of its budget, especially in the appropriation for salaries and expenses (Table V-1). During the period 1966-1975, domestic positions have consistently totaled around 300, whereas the salary and expense appropriation has nearly doubled from 2.48 million dollars to 4.70 million dollars. Activities funded by this appropriation include administration, engineering, surveying, and operation and maintenance. The latter activity alone accounted for 72.4 percent of the 1974 salary and expense appropriation.

Much more widely fluctuating than the appropriation for salaries and expenses is the funding for construction activities (Table V-2). Construction appropriations finance projects dealing with sanitation, flood control, boundary location and relocation, and water salinity. These projects are generally undertaken in response to treaty obligations. For instance, $48,428,000 of the 1975 construction budget, nearly half of the total, is earmarked for the Colorado River Salinity Project that was designated by treaty in 1973.

TABLE V-1

Salary and Expense Appropriations, U.S. Section, 1966-1975

YEAR	DOMESTIC POSITIONS	AMOUNT	YEAR	DOMESTIC POSITIONS	AMOUNT
1966	304	$2,480,000	1971	322	$3,788,000
1967	288	2,836,000	1972	307	3,999,000
1968	287	2,786,000	1973	300	4,190,000
1969	337	2,952,000	1974	298	4,595,000
1970	325	3,507,520	1975 est.	298	4,701,000

Source: U.S. Department of State, 1974: 26.

TABLE V-2

Construction Appropriations, U.S. Section, 1966-1975

YEAR	DOMESTIC POSITIONS	AMOUNT	YEAR	DOMESTIC POSITIONS	AMOUNT
1966	103	$10,883,000	1971	35	$ 4,200,000
1967	67	5,754,000	1972	32	6,280,000
1968	89	9,000,000	1973	32	20,246,000
1969	114	5,806,000	1974	72	3,800,000
1970	16	411,629	1975 est.	278	102,306,000

Source: U.S. Department of State, 1974: 27.

VI

Boundary Adjustment Through Banco Elimination

Although Commissioners Mills and Osorno petitioned their governments in 1895 to amend existing treaties in order to eliminate bancos, a similar proposal had already been offered eight years earlier by a frustrated customs collector at Brownsville, Texas. J. J. Cocke in a letter to his congressman relayed the difficulties of his office in collecting duties and retarding smuggling along the lower Rio Grande. Criminals and smugglers found the meander cutoffs natural refuges from authorities on either side of the River who intentionally avoided international incidents by exercising little or no jurisdiction in the vicinity of bancos. Cocke also realized that the rounds made by his mounted inspectors were becoming increasingly longer as bancos developed, and that the boundary itself was lengthening in a sinuous pattern. He recommended that the United States should assume jurisdiction on all bancos attached to the north bank of the River; Mexico would do likewise on the south bank. The evidence presented by him in his correspondence led him to conclude that:

> The so called "Morteritos Treaty" of Nov. 12, 1884 proclaimed Sept. 14, 1886 is perfectly worthless. Though framed apparently for the express purpose of defining the boundary, it does not do it any more effectively than the former treaty. . . . Who is to determine where the old bed's middle is? When there are two or three old beds, how is it to be decided which was abandoned by the river before 1852 and which since? (Cocke to Crain, 1887 in Chamizal, U.S. *Appendix*, 1911: 694-95).

Seven years after Cocke's letter, in the fall of 1894, the Commission met in El Paso, but decided to reassemble in Laredo on the lower Rio Grande in order to investigate complaints related to the numerous banco cases along that portion of the River. An on-the-spot inspection of the bancos, reviews of engineering and survey reports, plus testimony of witnesses, prompted Commissioner Mills to record that:

These bancos are typical of all the rest, not having been in any way selected, but taken at random by the accident of the complaints. There are perhaps forty or forty-five other bancos of a similar character, probably nearly equally distributed on the two banks of the river between Rio Grande City and the Gulf. They will likely have but an average of one or two hundred yards frontage on the river channel, but the length of boundary added by following the deepest channel in the bayou or old river bed will probably average four or five miles, thus increasing the boundary line several hundred miles, which, instead of simplifying the boundary question, will confound the confusion already existing (Mills to Secretary of State, in *Proceedings,* 1903: 175).

Several immediate problems arose which restrained the commissioners from applying the Treaty of 1884 and making an award. For instance, after a banco is formed avulsively the River might shift more slowly, leaving a strip of accretion deposits between the base of the cutoff and the active channel. Where this occurs, a banco becomes an enclave completely surrounded by the domain of another country. In the case of Banco de Santa Rita, the Mexican owner was granted a right-of-way to the River by authorities in Texas. He fenced his right-of-way across the accretion strip to the River, bisecting a parcel of land owned by a United States citizen. The latter then applied to the Commission for a right-of-way across the Mexican's right-of-way!

Even if it were assumed that every banco initially forms through avulsion, what happens should the River encroach on the banco at a later date, leaving an accretion strip fronting the River? If the accretions are awarded to the owners adjacent to the banco, would the active international boundary shift away from the banco, leaving the tract as an enclave surrounded by another country's jurisdiction and without the access to the River it formerly possessed? If, on the other hand, these accretions are awarded to the banco tract, would the active boundary remain unchanged in the old channel where the River fronts bancos, and shift where it does not? According to Mills:

In the cases of the Banco de Grangeno and Santa Margarita, this was the sole question for our consideration; the parties raising no question as to the jurisdiction of Mexico over bancos proper, but the whole question being a dispute over some thirty or forty acres of accretion; the proprietor of the banco claiming it as against the owner of the adjacent land. In all these cases the reverse of Mr. Cushing's proposition appears true, and that the nation would suffer greater injury by the loss of the natural river boundary than the loss of territory (Mills to Secretary of State, in *Proceedings,* 1903: 175).

Banco de Grangeno was located approximately seven miles upstream of Hidalgo and Reynosa. According to witnesses, the banco formed in 1870 by an avulsive cut that shortened the River by four or five miles (Fig. VI-1). The long axis of the banco measured nearly two miles at the time of banco formation. In the succeeding twelve years the River encroached on the base of the banco approximately 0.75 miles, then gradually withdrew southeastward, leaving an accretion strip approximately 1000 feet wide between the banco and the active channel. All witnesses called before the Commission in 1894 appear to have offered consistent testimony regarding an avulsive change in 1870, encroachment in 1882, and subsequent withdrawal and accretion by 1894.

Banco investigation proved costly in time and money. In the case of Grangeno Banco, the Commission had accurate boundary and River maps from the 1853 Emory-Salazar survey and the 1894 Commission survey. The determination of the River's position during the intermediate period was more difficult. Witnesses and field evidence eventually supplied the channel traces for 1870 and 1882. A fence had long occupied the middle of the channel abandoned in 1870. Also, a lagoon or segment of the 1882 channel still filled with water was mapped by the Commission and its origin verified by witnesses (Mills and Osorno, in *Proceedings,* 1903: 183-85). Of immense value was the one meter contour interval used on the survey map of 1894. Traces of the old channel are unmistakable on the maps where topographic lows form conspicuous arcs in the landscape.

Farther downstream between Rosario, Texas and Rosario, Tamaulipas, the Commission investigated the Santa Margarita Banco. It was more complex than Grangeno Banco in that it was a double banco with two sections of post-avulsion accretion deposits. As in the case of Grangeno Banco, the Commission reached no accord on the assignment and disposition of these banco-accretion deposits.

These problems led Osorno and Mills to suggest that banco jurisdiction be transferred to the country to which the banco becomes attached, provided that the length of the banco's long axis is greater than the length of the banco's river frontage. It is not clear why they specified a geometric limit for the bancos to be eliminated by their proposal. Perhaps all of the problem bancos they had inspected would have been eliminated. More likely, they recognized that once the ratio of frontage to length of long axis exceeds unity, the implication is that the River has already severely encroached on the banco and further encroachment will obliterate the tract in question.

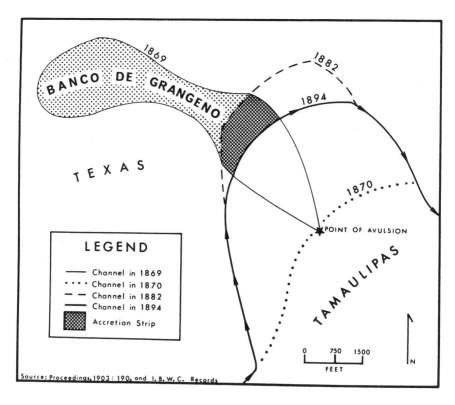

FIGURE VI-1. *An early banco case where a portion of the banco was obliterated by subsequent river erosion and replaced by accretion deposits.*

Treaty of 1905

In anticipation of a new treaty dealing with bancos, the Commission decided to survey and map existing bancos along the lower Rio Grande below its confluence with the Rio San Juan. By 1898, studies of fifty-eight bancos were complete, but still no treaty to deal with the disposition of the troublesome enclaves. Negotiations between the United States and Mexico over the possible exchange of banco territory apparently stalled because the Mexican Constitution forbade the transfer of Mexican soil to another country. This constitutional problem was not circumvented until 1905, at which time negotiators substituted "transfer of jurisdiction" for "transfer of territory" in the text of their treaty (Fig. VI-2).

Article 1 of the Treaty of 1905 exempted the previously mentioned fifty-eight bancos from the provisions of the Treaty of 1884 that required the boundary to follow the old channel around a banco which was avulsively formed. The Treaty of 1905 does not, however, invalidate Cushing's 1856 opinion and that portion of international law on which the 1884 Treaty was based. Instead it represents the first time by treaty where the United States and Mexico recognized the Rio Grande as a very special international river requiring very special regulations. It also involves the first treaty between the two countries to be based on recommendations of local officials, rather than on the whims of Washington politicians who had never inspected the treaty area. Article 1 also solved the problem of banco jurisdiction by providing that:

... the boundary line between the two countries shall ... follow the deepest channel of the stream — and the dominion and jurisdiction of so many of the ... *bancos* as may remain on the right bank of the river shall pass to Mexico, and the dominion and jurisdiction of those ... *bancos* which may remain on the left bank shall pass to the United States of America (35 Stat. 1863).

Other bancos, those not already surveyed and those which might form in the future, were to be eliminated in the same manner. Fortunately, the treaty did not place a geometric limit on bancos as the commissioners had proposed. However, the treaty does contain a provision that exempts very large or highly populated tracts from elimination. According to Article 2 of the 1905 Treaty:

There are hereby excepted from this provision the portions of land segregated by the change in the bed of the said rivers having an area of over two hundred and fifty (250) hectares, or a population of over two hundred (200) souls, and which shall not be considered as *bancos* for the purposes of this treaty and shall not be eliminated, the old bed of the river remaining, therefore, the boundary in such cases (35 Stat. 1863).

In other words, these large tracts would have to be awarded on the basis of the Treaties of 1884 and 1889, and the boundary would follow the dry channel around tracts that were formed through avulsion. A question arises as to what prompted the treaty makers into letting a portion of the river boundary go dry, and allowing a few large tracts of land to be awarded on the basis of treaties which had already

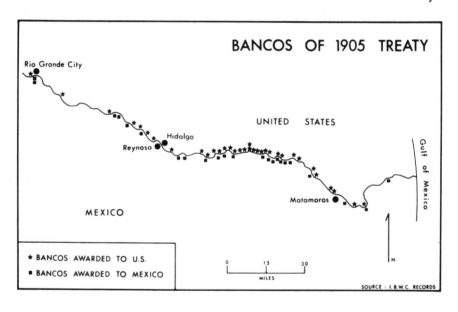

FIGURE VI-2. *Distribution of the initial fifty-eight lower Rio Grande bancos eliminated by the Treaty of 1905.*

proven themselves ineffective. The answer (and this is speculation) might lie in the contested Chamizal tract in south El Paso which first came to the Commission's attention in 1894, and on whose jurisdiction the commissioners never agreed. By the time the Treaty of 1905 was signed, Mexico had been through a decade of Chamizal negotiations, and likely would not let the valuable parcel of land slip away via treaty (Chapter VII).

That the treaty makers had little knowledge of the behavior of meandering alluvial streams is evident in Article 3 of the 1905 Treaty:

> On all separated land on which the successive alluvium deposits have caused to disappear those parts of the abandoned channel which are adjacent to the river, each of the extremities of said channel shall be united by means of a straight line to the nearest part of the bank of the same river (35 Stat. 1863).

The drafters of the provision did not realize how tight the bends of some meanders become just prior to avulsion. While some meanders in the Rio Grande have a typical horseshoe shape, others become even tighter and are referred to as "goosenecks." If the ends of a gooseneck banco become obliterated by accretion deposits, and straight lines are drawn from the ends of the visible dry channel to the river bank, the lines would cut across "old ground outside the banco-ground which had always formed a part of the mainland" (Follett and Zayas to their Commissioners, in *Elimination of Bancos*, First Series, 1910: 19). Although a few banco cases were settled by circumventing the treaty and approximating the trace of the banco's channel ends, the Commission in later years complied with the treaty's provision of lines drawn perpendicular to the bank (Fig. VI-3).

A case where the commissioners circumvented the 1905 Treaty is Tortuga Banco No. 65. It lies north of the Rio Grande some fifteen miles upstream of Hidalgo, and was claimed by a United States citizen who bought the Mexican title (Fig. VI-4). Surveys in 1910 confirmed that this banco was cut from Mexico around 1860, and it was identified by a short section of old channel around an island-like piece of higher ground that supported several old mesquite trees. During the intervening fifty years, the River shifted in a large arc away from the banco and added accretion deposits both to the banco-land and to adjacent Texas soil. It is evident from the map that lines drawn perpendicular from the modern bank to the visible ends of the dry channel would give the banco much more land than would be indicated by the spirit of the 1905 Treaty.

If a traverse were laid running from the end of the old channel to the nearest points on the river's bank, it would give the banco 2,000 meters river frontage and would cut square across accretion which belongs to the adjacent main land, not disturbed by the river. In this dilemma, we assumed intermediate positions for the river. We knew that when the banco cut off the river must have run about at right angles to the banco. This,

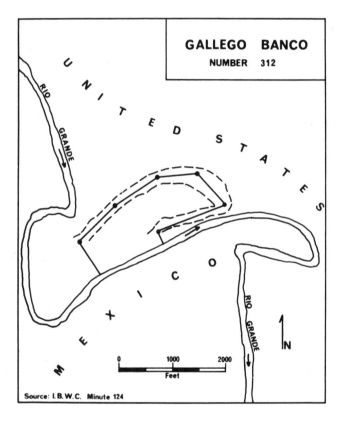

FIGURE VI-3. *An illustration of the method prescribed in the 1905 Treaty for surveying a banco whose channel ends are not wholly visible. The dry channel ends are linked to the River by a set of survey lines drawn perpendicular to the active bank.*

together with the old banks, enabled us to locate Cors. 4 and 8. We then assumed that the river would begin to curve as it moved south, and we located Cors. 3 and 9, running courses 4-3 and 8-9 as near as we could determine, at right angles to this intermediate course of the river. We had the position of the 1898 bank and put Cors. 2 and 10 on it, making corners 3-2 and 9-10 at right angles to it. Then we went to the present river, striking its normal bank at right angles. (Follett and Zayas to their Commissioners, in *Elimination of Bancos*, Second Series, 1911: 16).

Finally, the Treaty of 1905 provided for rights of citizens who might find their banco-land under the jurisdiction of another country. According to Article 4, citizens could either sell or retain their banco-land. If they chose to reside on it, they could keep their existing citizenship, or acquire the citizenship of the country to which their land had become attached.

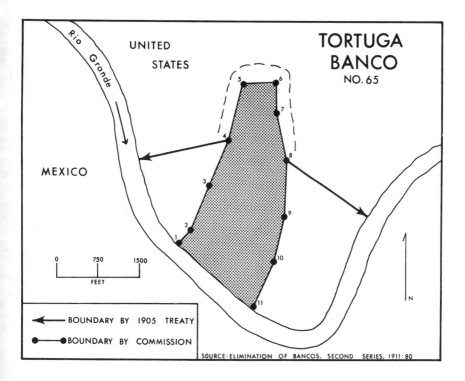

FIGURE VI-4. *A banco case where survey lines circumvented those prescribed by treaty in order to divide accretion deposits equitably.*

Problems and Procedures

Between the end of the original banco surveys in 1898 and the sign-ing of the 1905 Treaty, the Rio Grande had encroached on and re-worked many of the bancos. A few bancos were entirely eliminated by erosion subsequent to the surveys, while one previously unde-tected banco was found. The Estrada Banco, cut from Mexico in 1897, had been completely removed and replaced by accretion de-posits. Consulting engineers in 1909 found no trace of the banco or of its dry channel.

The Estrada Banco is interesting in that it was not a true banco in the sense of being a cutoff meander, but rather, it had been a large sand bar that forced the River to bifurcate into two channels, with the major channel against the United States bank. In 1897, the River abandoned the north channel in favor of the south channel, and the Mexican sand bar became attached to the United States shore. There-fore, the evidence normally used to establish that a banco is old ground, i.e., trees, soil horizons, fences, cultivation, occupance, etc., was not present when the Boundary Commission mapped this thirty-two acre tract and its dry channel. Here we have a case where a par-cel of land was treated as a banco in order to establish rightful juris-diction according to law, although the term "banco" itself is generally restricted to meanders cut off by avulsive changes.

The small size of the Estrada Banco does not alone account for its having been subsequently destroyed by erosion and replaced by ac-cretion. Because the sand bar was composed of young channel al-luvium of loose consistency, it seems likely that it could not resist erosion as well as older bancos that had had the opportunity to com-pact their sediments and anchor themselves by vegetative growth. When mapped, the Estrada Banco had a long axis of 1000 feet per-pendicular to the River. This means that the mean annual rate of erosion and accretion during the period 1897-1909 was a minimum of 85 feet in the vicinity of the banco (*Proceedings*, 1903: 200, 204, 222). Add to this the fact that the moderate and high flows that generate channel-forming processes persist for only a few weeks each year, and one can conclude that the rate of channel migration in the vicinity of

Estrada Banco during short periods of time must have been several times greater than the mean annual rate. It is doubtful that shifts in channel position at a rate comparable to that which occurred at Estrada Banco can be regarded as accretion as defined in classic international law, for it is unlikely that the changes were slow and gradual or imperceptible at given points in time. This case illustrates the conflict between how international law believes rivers should behave, and how some rivers, such as the Rio Grande, actually do behave.

The task of determining the precise location of the boundary in the vicinity of bancos subject to elimination was not an easy one. In several cases, Boundary Commission surveyors discovered that portions of the dry banco channel had become obliterated by accretion deposits which had formed after the surveys of the late 1890's. These deposits indicated recent River encroachment on the bancos and the temporary use of the banco channels during flood stage. Of great aid to the surveyors and engineers were the old fences that had been erected in the original dry channels by ranchers and farmers. Cottonwood fence posts proved especially helpful, for instead of rotting in the moist bottom lands, they often regenerated into an arc of towering trees whose trace unmistakably demarcated the old channel. In ten of the first fifty-eight bancos eliminated, cottonwood trees and mesquite posts were used to determine the boundary (Follett and Zayas to their Commissioners, in *Elimination of Bancos,* First Series, 1910: 20-24).

Once a banco is reported to the Commission, it is the duty of the principal engineers to survey the banco and map it at a scale of 1:-5000. Usually the survey is run by the country to which the banco is attached. If there is a question of exact location and date of formation, the engineers usually hold a hearing and take testimony from witnesses. Should such testimony conflict with any of the topographical evidence, it is usually discarded, and the banco is demarcated on survey evidence only.

Of special interest is the case of Solisenito Banco No. 81, located on the lower Rio Grande between Hidalgo and Brownsville, and claimed in 1910 by a Mexican citizen, Filomeno Garcia. At first glance, this banco appears on a map to be Mexican soil, having been transferred to the north of the River in 1887 by a cutoff or avulsion (Fig. VI-5). However, the United States consulting engineer firmly believed that this land was actually part of an older banco that cut from Texas to Mexico in 1865, then returned to the Texas side, greatly enlarged by accretion, through a second avulsion in 1887. The remainder of the 1865 banco, according to the Texas claimant Josiah Turner, still lay south of the River.

Because topographic evidence for an older banco section south of the River was essentially lacking, the consulting engineers of the Boundary Commission resorted to verbal testimony to establish the boundary. Turner testified that:

> . . . I desire to say that in the year of 1865 after the first overflow of the Rio Grande, a part of the Galveston Ranch, which at that time belonged to my father-in-law, Don Anastacio Trevino, was cut off and thrown onto the Mexican side — about forty acres of the upper potrero. The land was recognized as Don Anastacio's even after being thrown to the Mexican side. Don Anastacio, however, borrowed a hundred dollars from Jesus Garcia, and let Jesus use the land for agricultural purposes in the meantime. When Jesus Garcia died, I personally paid to his widow the hundred dollars which had been borrowed by Anastacio, and I immediately took possession of the piece then on the Mexican side.
>
> Afterwards Emilio Fernandez contracted to buy it from me for two hundred dollars (Anastacio being dead and I being in charge of his affairs), but paid me but one hundred. Then for a long time he refused to pay me the balance, feeling that as the banco was on Mexican territory but under American jurisdiction, it would be hard for me to enforce my rights.
>
> About 1885 or 1886 the river took another cut and threw almost the entire banco onto the Texas side again, leaving a few acres only on the Mexican side. Immediately upon seeing my own land coming by to me through nature's agency, I took possession of it and have held ever since. (Follett to Mills, in *Elimination of Bancos*, Second Series, 1911: 53).

Turner's stepson Venturia Longoria and several Mexican witnesses all supported Turner's testimony of two avulsions, but all equally testified that the older banco cut in 1865 was totally destroyed by erosion and replaced by accretion prior to the avulsion of 1887. In other words, the land transferred to the Texas side of the River in 1887 was young Mexican alluvium and not old Texas soil.

No doubt, 1865 was a year of unusually high discharges, flooding, and banco cutting along much of the Rio Grande (Chapter VIII). In addition to the initial Solisenito Banco, Antonio Vela, San Pedro, and San Miguel Bancos were also cut in 1865 along the lower Rio Grande, and a significant portion of the Chamizal tract at El Paso was being formed at the same time (Chapter VII). Interestingly, the original Solisenito Banco was entirely destroyed by erosion and replaced by accretion during the period 1865- 1887. If all of the 1887 Solisenito Banco was cut from young alluvium deposited in the previous twenty-two years, then the rate of lateral accretion during the 1865-1887 period was well over 100 feet per year. Here, as in the case of the Estrada Banco mentioned earlier, much of the change cannot be re-garded as simple accretion as defined in international law.

The commissioners met in 1911 and inspected the Solisenito Banco. They examined previous testimony, requestioned Turner, and found no traces of abandoned channels south of the River with which to substantiate Turner's claim. As a result, Commissioner Mills sided with the Mexican engineer and Commission, and Solisenito was to be eliminated as a Mexican banco. Noting Turner's inability to sup-ply concrete information, the commissioners concluded that:

... it was not necessary to take testimony in this case as their own exami-nation of the physical condition of the land, together with the maps, made it possible for them to arrive at a decision, especially as it had always been the experience of the Commissioners that testimony of witnesses as to the movements of the river even for a short period back, was almost wholly unreliable. (Mills and Puga, Joint Journal of March 27, 1911, in *Elimina-tion of Bancos,* 1911: 48).

The numbers assigned to bancos refer to general location only, and may or may not suggest a date of banco formation. For instance, all bancos on the lower Rio Grande have numbers between 1 and 156. The first fifty-eight bancos eliminated by the Treaty of 1905 are num-bered consecutively, beginning with Burrita Banco No. 1 near the Gulf and extending upstream to Yzaguirre Banco No. 58 at Rio Gran-de City. All of the original fifty-eight bancos formed between 1850 and 1900. Banco numbers higher than 58 on the lower Rio Grande usually suggest a post-1900 formation, except for cases where older bancos escaped previous surveys. For example, Santa Anita No. 86 formed in 1881 and San Pedro No. 87 formed in 1865.

Banco names are generally taken from claimants or occupants of the tract, or from nearby geographic points. Examples of the former type of name include Dougherty, Zolezzi, Saenz, and Celaya Bancos; examples with geographic names include Jalisco, Santa Rosalia, San Francisco, and Monterrey Bancos. Once surveyed and named, these bancos are listed on the Commission Minutes for elimination. If the Minutes are approved by the United States Department of State and the Mexican Ministry of Foreign Relations, elimination is carried into effect (I.B.W.C. *Report,* Revised 1954: 73-74).

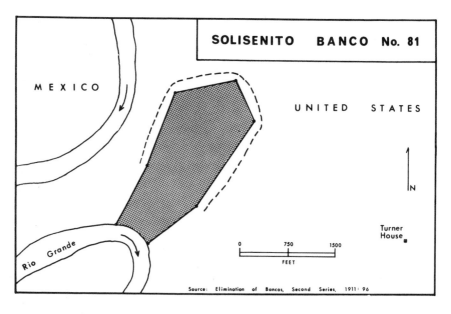

FIGURE VI-5. *An 1887 banco of young Mexican alluvium occupying the site of an older 1865 banco cut from the United States.*

Bancos Eliminated

The signing of the 1905 Treaty automatically eliminated the fifty-eight bancos mentioned in the treaty. Of these, Nos. 50 and 54 had eliminated themselves by erosion between 1898 and 1905. Also included in this series is the sizeable Fernandez Banco, No. 4 1/2, cut from the United States in 1860, but undetected in the original Mills-Osorno surveys.

Another large series of thirty-one bancos in the lower Rio Grande was eliminated between 1910 and 1912. During the succeeding decade the Commission was inactive, with Mexican governments unstable, and United States-Mexican relations generally strained. Mills summarized the Commission's activity before 1912 as follows:

> During the sixteen years of our active service (the revolution in Mexico in 1911 having put an end to our activities), the Commission tried over one hundred cases of all kinds, disagreeing only in the Chamizal case, and preserved the peace and quiet of the entire Rio Grande border for these long years . . . (Mills, 1921: 297).

In 1922 the Commission was reactivated with the appointment of George Curry as United States Commissioner. Curry was replaced on the Commission in 1927 by L. M. Lawson. By 1928, both sections of the Boundary Commission had completed surveys of the forty-two bancos on the lower Rio Grande which had formed since 1912. This third series of bancos, Nos. 90-131, was eliminated in 1928. Also eliminated at this time were the only two banco cases ever to be dealt with on the short Colorado River segment of the international boundary.

Banco surveys were also begun on other troublesome reaches of the Rio Grande. In 1930, nineteen bancos were eliminated in the El Paso-Juarez Valley. By 1932, a twentieth banco was eliminated, providing the last banco case ever for this section of the River. The rapid decline in the number of banco cases in the El Paso-Juarez Valley reflects the flood control and reservoir measures undertaken in southern New Mexico, plus the rectification of the channel in the vicinity of El Paso.

Since 1930 there have been few large series of bancos eliminated. Another twenty-five cases have been settled on the lower Rio Grande.

Of these, only one was eliminated after 1949, the Los Indios Banco cut in 1967 and eliminated the following year. In 1944, twelve bancos were eliminated in the Quitman Canyon just downstream from the El Paso-Juarez Valley. A year later the Quitman Canyon's last banco case was resolved. Also in 1945, eleven bancos were eliminated in the Presidio Valley. This valley had another twenty-one bancos cut between 1860 and 1927 on which no agreement was reached until 1970. These bancos will likely become the last large series ever to be eliminated on the Rio Grande.

TABLE VI-1

Summary of Bancos Eliminated 1905-1970

BANCO SERIAL NUMBER	LOCATION	CUT TO UNITED STATES NO.	ACRES	CUT TO MEXICO NO.	ACRES	TOTAL NO.	ACRES
	RIO GRANDE:						
1-156	Lower Rio Grande	89	11,487.0	66	8,227.0	155	19,714.0
301-320	El Paso Valley	16	3,140.1	4	417.5	20	3,557.6
321-333	Quitman Canyon	12	253.7	1	55.3	13	309.0
401-450	Presidio Valley	21	1,988.5	28	2,962.1	49	4,950.6
601-602	Hill Section	2	793.5	----	----	2	793.5
	TOTAL: Rio Grande	140	17,662.8	99	11,661.9	239	29,324.7
501-502	COLORADO RIVER	2	842.4	----	----	2	842.4
	TOTALS	142	18,505.2	99	11,661.9	241	30,167.1

Source: I.B.W.C. records.

In summary, the Commission has eliminated 239 bancos on the Rio Grande between 1905-1970 (Table VI-1). Of these, 140 were severed from Mexico and passed to the United States; the remaining 99 bancos cut from the United States passed to Mexico. Most of the total banco area of 29,324.7 acres, some 60.2 percent, has passed to the United States. Barring some serious strain in United States-Mexican relations, or a catastrophic flood, there will be no large series of banco cases to be settled in the future. Individual cases of the banco type may likely appear on the lower Rio Grande. These will probably be dealt with individually in accordance with the 1970 Treaty that supersedes the 1905 Treaty (Chapter X).

VII

Chamizal

W Although the Rio Grande has a constricted channel in west El
Paso where it abuts Cerro de Cristo Rey, the River changes
character rapidly in south El Paso. Here the River changes course
from southeast to almost due east, and enters the broad alluvial El
Paso-Juarez Valley. Here too is the uppermost reach along which
boundary problems have arisen. A hint of the havoc the River would
play in disrupting the international boundary occurred as early as
1852 when two surveys conducted several months apart by the
Emory-Salazar Commission showed a slight southward shift in the
channel's position (Chamizal, U.S. *Appendix*, 1911: 109). By 1889
the channel was far south of its 1852 position, in some places as much
as a mile (Fig. VII-1). The tract of land between the old and the new
channel, some 600 acres, found itself attached to south El Paso at the
expense of north Juarez. Named for the brush patch that formerly
covered the area, the tract was locally known as *El Chamizal* (Liss,
1965: 1). The parcel developed and grew over a period of forty-three
years; it was brought to the Boundary Commission's attention as early
as 1895. After 1895 the River migrated a short distance northward,
and by 1907 was eroding the southern end of the tract. In general,
Chamizal can be defined as that area lying between the old 1852 and
the younger active channel, regardless of the latter's position.

Pre-arbitral Efforts of Resolution 1895-1910

In 1827, a Mexican citizen obtained title to the area that included
Chamizal. Upon his death in 1866, the tract was willed to his grand-
son, Pedro Garcia. Nearly thirty years later, in 1895, Garcia made a
formal complaint to the Mexican Boundary Commissioner over jurisdiction for Chamizal. Obviously familiar with the Treaty of 1884, Garcia claimed that the tract was formed by an "abrupt and sudden

change of current" which in 1873 severed the tract from Mexico and attached it to south El Paso. Why had he not occupied the land or sought jurisdictional status during the intervening twenty-two years? Supposedly he had feared retaliation from United States citizens and was concerned about property taxes (Chamizal, U.S. *Appendix,* 1911: 104-05).

The commissioners had little difficulty in accepting the problem as one within their jurisdiction to be resolved in accordance with the Treaties of 1884 and 1889. A survey, a map, and the determination of whether the channel shift was avulsive or slow and gradual would decide the case. The report of the Mexican consulting engineer in

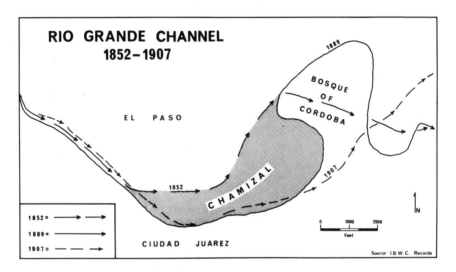

FIGURE VII-1. *Positions of the Rio Grande channel in the upper El Paso-Juarez Valley. Note the location of the Chamizal tract between the 1852 and active channels.*

1896 inhibited a simple settlement. He concluded that the River had abandoned its Emory-Salazar channel already in 1852, not in 1873 as implied by Garcia's statement. Furthermore, the shift was avulsive and precipitated a whole series of southward avulsions that culminated in the great floods of 1864-68 that brought the channel to its approximate 1895 position (Chamizal, U.S. *Appendix*, 1911: 182-83). Commissioner Mills argued that there was not sufficient physical evidence to prove that the entire shift was due to avulsion; neither were maps available to show the channel's position during the 1860's and 1870's. Without reaching an accord, the commissioners sent a report of their findings to their respective governments, and recorded their views in a Joint Journal.

In terms of the Treaty of 1884, and based on Cushing's 1856 opinion, the contrasting views of the commissioners in the Chamizal controversy cannot be faulted. As mentioned in Chapter IV, the Treaty of 1884 has provisions related only to the extremes in processes of channel change, rather than to the full range in processes. The Mexican Commissioner assumed that, since the Treaty of 1884 mentions a boundary shift only in conjunction with a "slow and gradual" channel shift, no other type of channel change can affect the boundary. He considered the episodic shift of the Rio Grande, as reported by his engineer, not to have had any effect on the boundary. Commissioner Mills countered that seven witnesses before the Commission all testified that the River had never overflowed its banks in the Chamizal area; hence, how was it possible for a new channel to be cut, and for an old one to be abandoned? Therefore, he applied the term *avulsion* as it was defined in the Treaty of 1884 and accordingly dismissed it as the process responsible for Chamizal. Hence, he regarded the fluvial boundary as mobile and in a state of constant flux, with a permanent boundary line established only when an old channel is abandoned. He also quoted from Vattel that, where doubt exists as to jurisdiction and channel changes along a boundary, it is better for the interested parties to keep the river as their natural boundary.

Mills, in an obvious attempt to bolster the position of the United States, tried to weaken the Mexican contention of rapid erosion by emphasizing the average annual shift of the River between 1852 and

1895. Mexico claimed that "slow and gradual" refers to the rate of the process (erosion), while Mills argued that "slow and gradual" refers to the long-term effect of the process. Commissioner Mills used the figures calculated by the Mexican engineer that the average annual shift of the River was 32.57 meters. Testimony of witnesses put the emphasis back on the frequency and magnitude of the process, rather than on some meaningless average. Residents both of El Paso and of Juarez confirmed that little or no change occurred in the channel's position from 1852 to 1864; rapid changes accompanied large floods from 1864-68; little or no change occurred after 1868 (Chamizal, U.S. *Appendix*, 1911: 201-13). Thus, if the net channel movement were restricted to the five-year period of 1864-1868, the shift would have occurred at a rate of nearly 280 meters per year. Taking into account the fact that the River had little or no flow during half the year, the rate of bank erosion during periods of actual flow was equivalent to approximately 560 meters per year, or nearly five feet per day. It is difficult to assess this rate of change as accretion, i.e., as erosion of one bank with equivalent deposition on the other, if accretion be defined in terms of perceptibility of the process. Furthermore, a witness appeared before the Boundary Commission and testified that:

In 1864 the current was so strong as to destroy the jetties constructed on the Mexican side of the river, going behind them and this prevented the river from going back to its old channel. The changes were to such a degree that at times during the night the river would wear away from 50 to 100 yards. There were instances in which people living in houses distant 50 yards from the banks, on one evening had to fly in the morning from the place on account of the encroachments of the river and on many occasions they had no time to cut down their wheat or other crops. It carried away forests without giving time to the people to cut the trees down. There are never changes during the Winter. (Doctor Mariano Samaniego quoted in Chamizal, U.S. *Appendix*, 1911: 190).

In 1896 the unsettled Chamizal case was closed in order that the Commission might move ahead with other cases and complaints. A year later the commissioners asked their governments to reopen and resolve the Chamizal dispute because of its interference with bridge construction between El Paso and Juarez. They also suggested that a third commissioner be added to serve as arbiter. The United States agreed; Mexico refused. Mexico contended that although the Commission functioned to decide awards, the United States Department of State and the Mexican Ministry of Foreign Relations actually finalized them. Therefore, the Mexican Government refused to be bound to the decision of a commissioner who "could be nothing more than a private individual" (Chamizal, U.S. *Appendix*, 1911: 347-53). After an exchange of rejected proposals on how to add an arbiter, the Commission dropped Chamizal from negotiation in 1898.

A reasonable method of settling Chamizal was proposed in 1908 by Mexico as part of a boundary rectification package. The United States would get El Chamizal and the adjacent Bosque of Cordoba (Mexican) in exchange for the bar of El Horcon (U.S.) and a large United States island of fertile floodplain soil in the El Paso-Juarez Valley (Fig. VII-1 and Fig. X-2). The United States refused by stating that it agreed in principle, but that the Mexican theory was:

. . . entirely inconsistent with the course of the two governments during many years, and particularly with the attitude of the Mexican government toward the Chamizal Case . . . (Chamizal, U.S. *Appendix*, 1911: 397).

Mexico then urged arbitration. In 1910 there was signed a Convention of Arbitration based on an earlier 1907 Mexican proposal of adding a Canadian jurist to the Commission. The jurist's primary function was to cast deciding votes on all issues in the Chamizal case not agreed upon by the commissioners. As a result:

The decision of the Commissioners, whether rendered unanimously or by majority vote of the Commissioners, shall be final and conclusive upon both governments, and without appeal (36 *Stat.*, 2481, 1910, Article 3).

Arbitration of 1911

The Arbitration Commission convened in May 1911, with Eugene Lafleur, a Canadian jurist, as presiding commissioner. Testimony and documents for each side were presented and reviewed for a full month. Eventually the number of primary issues was reduced to six, and a vote on and explanation of each was rendered by each of the three commissioners.

Mexico contended vigorously that the Chamizal case need not be settled by erosion versus avulsion, for according to Article 5 of the Treaty of 1848 and Article 1 of the Treaty of 1853, the boundary line was fixed and invariable. Thus, the true boundary was the boundary surveyed in 1852 by the Emory-Salazar Commission. The United States countered that both countries must have abandoned a fixed-line theory already in 1884 in order for them to sign a treaty, based on Cushing's opinion, that obviously regarded the boundary as a variable line (Chamizal, U.S. *Case*, 1911: 37). In addition, the United States argued that both countries must follow accepted principles of international law, including those principles related to mobile boundaries that were not specifically mentioned in the Treaties of 1848 and 1853. On the issue of a fixed-line theory, Commissioners Mills and Lafleur voted no; Mexican Commissioner Puga voted yes.

Another issue on which the Mexican Government claimed Chamizal was the non-retroactivity of the Treaty of 1884. Mexico claimed that the treaty was enacted to settle boundary problems subsequent to 1884, and therefore could not apply to Chamizal, which was essentially formed between 1852 and 1873. The United States readily proved that all negotiations entered into by the two governments concerning the Treaty of 1884 were prompted by boundary problems which had arisen since 1852, and hence, that the treaty was enacted to settle both existing and future boundary problems (Chamizal, U.S. *Countercase*, 1911: 1-20). On the issue of the retroactivity of the Treaty of 1884, Commissioners Mills and Lafleur voted yes; Commissioner Puga voted no (Chamizal Arbitration, *Award*, 1911: 34).

An interesting argument presented by the United States was that of prescription. International law recognizes the extension of sovereignty in cases where a tract of land is continuously occupied by a new sovereign, whose possession goes unchallenged by the former sovereign. The United States claimed uninterrupted occupation of Chamizal since 1836 on the basis of:

. . . the erection and maintenance of public buildings, railways, irrigation works, pavements, public sewers, residences, and business houses by the government of the United States, of the state of Texas, and of the citizens and inhabitants thereof (Chamizal, U.S. *Argument*, 1911: 116).

Mexico argued that its diplomatic correspondence in the preceding sixty years included requests for clarification of the boundary owing to channel changes, and therefore included Chamizal as an area of dispute and challenge. As a result, all three commissioners voted against prescription.

Three crucial issues arose, all relating to the manner in which Chamizal had formed. Both sides agreed that at times the River had shifted southward by a process neither slow and gradual, nor of outright channel abandonment. A thorough, unchallenged report of the behavior of the Rio Grande, especially in reference to the Chamizal's formation, was submitted by W. W. Follett, consulting engineer for the United States Section of the Boundary Commission. He concluded that:

"El Chamizal" was a level tract of land, above overflow, with a deep soil, inhabited, cultivated and covered with houses, orchards and vineyards. . . . Had an avulsive change occurred, the houses, vineyards and trees with the deep soil, would be found north of the river. Not a tree, house or vine was left. . . . There can be but one conclusion. . . . The river moved by erosion into the Chamizal tract and not by avulsion (Chamizal, U.S. *Countercase*, 1911: 233).

The United States also argued that the Treaty of 1884 mentions only one type of erosion (Chamizal Arbitration, *Award*, 1911: 37). Consequently, the boundary must shift regardless of whether the process of erosion is slow or rapid. In effect, Mills and the United States argued that although the Treaty of 1884 mentions only the *extremes* in processes, it also applies to the *ranges*. Therefore, it was contended that the same law that applies to slow erosion must also apply to rapid erosion.

Mexico countered that erosion as defined by the treaty is restricted by its modifiers of "slow and gradual." Proof that the Chamizal had formed by a process more rapid than "slow and gradual" was undisputable. Issue four was to determine if all of Chamizal had formed by slow and gradual erosion as defined in the Treaty of 1884. Mills voted yes, on the basis that the long-term effect of the process was slow and gradual even if the rate of the process was at times rapid. Puga and Lafleur voted no, on the basis that most of the tract formed by a process whose rate was much greater than that designated accretion in the Treaty of 1884. A logical consequence was to determine if part of Chamizal had formed by slow and gradual erosion. Lafleur and Puga voted that such was the case from 1852-1864, but not from 1864-1868 (Liss, 1965: 31). Mills abstained from voting on the latter two issues primarily because:

1. he foresaw a split of the tract;

2. he would not recognize for the period 1864-1868, a river process that was not specifically mentioned in the Treaty of 1884;

3. it was impossible to locate the position of the 1864 channel (Gregory, 1963: 23-25).

In June, 1911, Commissioner Lafleur issued the Chamizal Award. The United States would obtain title to all land north of the 1864 channel; Mexico would receive all land south of the 1864 channel (Chamizal Arbitration, *Award,* 1911: 35-36). Mexico, which would have received most of Chamizal, initially rejected the Award, as did the United States. Eventually Mexico accepted the Award, but Mills and the Department of State would not concede.

How could the United States legally reject an arbitration award? There are numerous precedents in international law where awards of arbitration tribunals can be rejected on the basis of: 1. awards excessively in favor of one party; 2. corruption of arbitrators; 3. awards not conforming to the guidelines of the convention of arbitration. Of these, Mills stressed the third, for the 1910 Convention for Arbitration states in Article III that "The Commission shall decide solely and exclusively as to whether the international title to the Chamizal tract is in the United States of America or Mexico" (36 Stat. 2481). Mills argued that the Commission was not empowered to divide the tract. Yet it can be argued that, as long as the award was made only to the two parties involved in the arbitration, and that the adverbs of "solely" and "exclusively" refer to the Commission's jurisdiction and *not* the title to the tract, a division of the tract was valid. While the balance of the ideas presented in this study are in accord with those of Gregory (1963), a leading student of the Chamizal issue whose research spanned several decades, this interpretation of Mills' position differs sharply.

In the case of the Chamizal, the subject in dispute was clearly defined, the question was clearly stated, and since the disputed tract was given neither to the United States nor to Mexico, the award rendered was outside of and beyond the terms of the Convention of 1910, which controlled the proceeding (Gregory, 1963: 32).

Another argument made by Mills in favor of rejection was his contention that the decision was impractical in that the 1864 channel could not be located. This argument was sound, inasmuch as engineers of both sections of the Boundary Commission had not found any trace of the River's 1864 position. However just was the division of the tract in the 1911 Award, it is unfortunate from an engineering standpoint that the judicial body designated as boundary a natural feature that no longer existed at the time the decision was rendered.

A last argument in favor of rejecting the award is the interpretation that "the commission has invented a third" process of channel change, namely rapid erosion (Utley, 1964: 119). This is nonsense, inasmuch as the Commission discovered an existing process that was not considered in treaty. Commissions detect processes, nature invents them, and international law might, as in the case of Chamizal, overlook them.

Hindsight suggests that, since the Treaty of 1884 was based essentially on the opinion of a United States Attorney General, it would have been a stroke of genius on the part of the United States to accept the Chamizal Award and to demand in return a simplified boundary treaty. It was, after all, the unworkability of the 1884 Treaty that led to the necessity for arbitration of the Chamizal case. Had the United States accepted the Award in 1911, it is unlikely that relations between the two countries would have been as disrupted and unfruitful as they were in succeeding decades, and much of the eventual cost of settling the Chamizal issue could have been prevented (Chapter IX).

Post-Arbitration Efforts at Resolution

Following the United States rejection of the Award, Chamizal became a national issue in Mexico where anti-imperialism sentiments ran high. During succeeding decades, newspapers exploited the case, and the tract's apparent value far surpassed its actual worth. Even worse,

While the governments of both nations struggled with negotiation problems, the Chamizal itself was growing. The population of the Chamizal was increasing, and capital investment in the area was rising despite the cloud on its title. More individuals became interested parties to the dispute, and Washington and Mexico City were deluged by requests to solve the title question (Liss, 1965: 37).

With the fall of President Porfirio Diaz and increasing domestic turmoil in Mexico in 1911, the United States proposed that the two countries review existing treaties and their interpretation in an effort to effect an agreement of convention which would amicably settle all

FIGURE VII-2. *This tract lying to the east of Chamizal was formed by an artificial cutoff in 1899 that increased channel efficiency and reduced the threat of floods.*

boundary problems related to channel changes. This proposal would have bypassed direct negotiation on Chamizal, but Mexico refused on the grounds that Chamizal was already awarded and not available for negotiation separately, or as part of a package proposal (U.S. *Foreign Relations,* 1911: 599).

Generally strained United States-Mexican relations during the decade following the award negated reasonable offers made by both sides. President Francisco Madero, successor to Diaz, offered to exchange Chamizal for the Island of San Elizario in the El Paso-Juarez Valley and Beaver Island (Morteritos) on the Lower Rio Grande. United States President Woodrow Wilson, an ardent foe of Madero, refused to negotiate. In 1913 the United States offered the bar of El Horcon in exchange for Chamizal and Cordova (Fig. VII-2). This proposal was very similar to the 1908 Mexican proposal, except that the United States excluded the Island of San Elizario which Mexico had sought in its earlier offer. At the same time, President Wilson refused to recognize the new regime of General Adolfo de la Huerta, who subsequently withdrew Chamizal from negotiation.

In 1932 United States Ambassador Clark and Mexican Minister Tellez agreed to a proposal which included: 1. rectification of the Rio Grande channel in the El Paso-Juarez Valley; 2. the transfer of Chamizal to the United States; 3. the transfer to Mexico, as part of rectification, of territory equal to that in the Chamizal zone between the 1864 and 1932 channels; 4. the release from the United States to Mexico of the Pious Fund and of Mexican debt to the Fund (Gregory, 1963: 37). The Pious Fund was originally begun in 1697 by the Catholic Church and the Spanish Government in support of California missions. The United States was awarded the Fund by the Hague Court in 1902, and Mexico was made liable for an annual payment of $43,050.99. Mexico had not paid since 1914. Had the items agreed to by Clark and Tellez been signed into treaty, it would have been necessary to first determine the actual or approximate position of the 1864 channel, in order to transfer, as part of rectification, the appropriate acreages to either side of the boundary. However, the failure of the two governments to agree on the location of the rectified channel in the vicinity of Chamizal led to a 1933 Treaty of Rectification which omitted from consideration both Chamizal and the Pious Fund. Significantly, rectification began about a mile east of Chamizal and proceeded downstream (Gregory, 1937: 294-301). The settlement of Chamizal was still three decades away.

The Chamizal and its resolution have been explored by a number of authors in greater detail than is offered here; but the brief coverage at this juncture and in Chapter IX is essential to the general discussion. The principal studies of Chamizal include Gregory (1937), Timm (1941), Gregory (1963), Liss (1965), and Fullerton (1968). Gladys Gregory compiled her original work under the direction of Dr. Charles Timm, longtime faculty member of the University of Texas. Frank Fullerton is Special Legal Assistant to the United States Section, International Boundary and Water Commission, and, like Stephen Liss, is a member of the State Department.

FIGURE VIII-1. *Aerial view of the Elephant Butte Dam and Reservoir Complex completed in 1916.*

VIII

Rectification and Flood Control

W Chamizal was not the only river-related problem in the El Paso-Juarez Valley at the turn of the century. The increasing demand for local agricultural products by the growing population on both sides of the Rio Grande increased the demand for regulated River flow, as did the continued disruption of agricultural production by periodic inundation, periodic drought, and shifts of the channel. About the same time, a dam was proposed to drain off flood waters for irrigation in the large Mesilla Valley of southern New Mexico, spelling potential disaster for the water-thirsty farmers of El Paso and Juarez.

While the 1905 Banco Treaty (Chapter VI) effectively reestablished the mobile River as boundary, the 1906 Water Allocation Treaty provided for the storage of flood waters that would be redistributed to irrigators both in the Mesilla and in the El Paso-Juarez Valleys. The 1906 Treaty provided for a dam and reservoir complex (Elephant Butte) to be built at Engle, New Mexico (Fig. VIII-1). The treaty also guaranteed Mexico 60,000 acre-feet of water annually to be delivered by the United States to the Old Mexican Canal (Acequia Madre) in Juarez. In return, Mexico waived all rights to excess Rio Grande water between the Juarez canal and Fort Quitman (35 Stat. 1863). The regulation of discharge should act to reduce the number of banco cases along the international boundary — as it has in fact done. In comparing the number of bancos cut in the El Paso-Juarez Valley during fifteen-year periods both before and after Elephant Butte, one finds twelve bancos cut between 1901 and 1915 and only three bancos cut between 1917 and 1931 (I.B.W.C. records, 1969).

Effect of Elephant Butte Dam on Discharge

Prior to the building of Elephant Butte, the Rio Grande conducted its highly variable discharge through a broad, shallow, and sinuous channel that traversed a series of alluvial valleys in southern New Mexico. With the completion of the dam complex in 1916, it was expected that the discharge through the alluvial valleys, including the El Paso-Juarez Valley, would be reduced both in magnitude and in variability. Hence, there would be fewer floods and channel movements to disrupt agriculture and the international boundary.

The effect of Elephant Butte Dam on Rio Grande discharge is self-evident when one examines a hydrograph for El Paso for periods before and after completion of the dam (Fig. VIII-2). Before the dam, daily discharge in early June averaged approximately 4,500 c.f.s.; after the dam, daily discharge in early June averaged 1,500 c.f.s. Also, the range in average daily discharge during the course of a calendar year was reduced from 4,200 c.f.s. before Elephant Butte to only 1,-300 c.f.s. after Elephant Butte. The variability of flow during the period 1915-27 was reduced by about 70 percent, whereas magnitude of flow on an annual basis was reduced by only 30 percent (Table VIII-1). The reduction of annual flow by 30 percent mostly reflects losses attributed to irrigation and to evaporation from reservoirs north of El Paso.

There are other tests of variability in flow before and after Elephant Butte. In 1904, twelve years before Elephant Butte, the total discharge at El Paso was 472,794 acre-feet, or approximately half the average annual volume of the 1890-1913 era. Some 453,065 acre-feet of the 1904 discharge, 96 percent, was recorded in just the last three months of the year (Ainsworth and Brown, 1933: 19). This figure is even more astounding when one considers that almost all the maximum mean daily discharges for El Paso during the period before Elephant Butte occurred in May and June, months associated with spring snow melt from mountains in the New Mexico watershed. Since 1916, most maximum mean daily discharges have been associated with late summer torrential rains falling between Elephant Butte and El Paso (Ainsworth and Brown, 1933: 21). Much of the change in seasonality of discharge can be attributed to the high capacity of reservoirs to absorb the spring runoff that follows on the heels of generally dry winters and springs.

Effect of Elephant Butte on Channel Morphology

Unknown to the engineers at the time of dam construction was the downstream effect on channel morphology that would be induced by a reservoir that not only regulated discharge, but also trapped most

TABLE VIII-1

Annual Discharge at El Paso in Acre-Feet

YEAR	DISCHARGE	YEAR	DISCHARGE	YEAR	DISCHARGE
1890	963,431	1922	780,029	1947	458,860
1891	1,929,160	1923	664,589	1948	431,680
1892	937,043	1924	799,071	1949	463,540
1897	1,357,267	1925	633,622	1950	472,630
1899	73,473	1926	556,941	1951	252,000
1900	169,668	1927	619,563	1952	283,680
1901	364,404	1928	624,400	1953	264,500
1902	50,759	1929	552,100	1954	93,725
1903	1,031,270	1930	532,700	1955	67,089
1904	472,794	1931	517,780	1956	57,481
1905	2,014,096	1932	567,240	1957	139,571
1906	1,116,612	1933	609,180	1958	392,863
1907	1,838,808	1934	508,490	1959	385,810
1908	466,882	1935	459,910	1960	378,260
1909	873,970	1936	473,800	1961	300,690
1910	580,162	1937	536,240	1962	376,116
1911	1,545,131	1938	554,900	1963	263,711
1912	1,360,896	1939	511,600	1964	64,307
1913	302,384	1940	453,900	1965	202,392
1916	594,530	1941	511,430	1966	308,782
1917	888,198	1942	1,559,200	1967	232,744
1918	348,951	1943	631,800	1968	264,408
1919	511,627	1944	611,900	1969	365,407
1920	709,778	1945	568,900	1970	360,719
1921	870,418	1946	497,900	1971	244,156
				1972	133,568
				1973	301,789

Source: Ainsworth and Brown, 1933: 19; I.B.W.C. *Water Bulletins* 12-36; I.B.W.C. Records.

of the River's sediment load. Between 1917 and 1932, the outflow from the dam recharged itself with sediment by scouring the bed of the channel approximately 1.63 feet in the alluvial valleys immediately downstream of Elephant Butte. During the same period, the average width of the River below the dam decreased from 612 feet to 466 feet. The extreme shallowness of the pre-1917 River is illustrated by the fact that the cross-sectional area of the channel just below Elephant Butte increased an average of 684 feet while width decreased by almost 24 percent. This increase in cross-sectional area can be attributed to increasing depth associated with scouring of the bed and the building up of the floodplain with sediment (Ainsworth and Brown, 1933: 12).

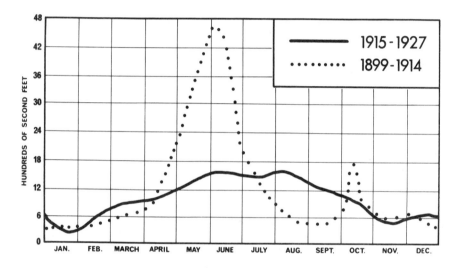

FIGURE VIII-2. *Hydrograph of mean daily discharge at El Paso for periods both before and after Elephant Butte Dam.*

Source: Ainsworth and Brown, 1933: Fig. 1.

Some of the scouring downstream of the dam was provoked by artificial cutoffs that locally increased the general gradient of 4 feet per mile. The decrease in the width-depth ratio and the shortening of the channel below Elephant Butte produced an increase in velocity and gradient, the net effect of which was to enhance scouring and sediment transport. Downstream from El Paso, where the channel gradient abruptly drops to only 2 feet per mile, the silt-laden River dumped much of its load. This aggradation was due not only to differences in gradient, but also to the fact that much surface water was drawn off for irrigation upstream of El Paso, with the result that the River's discharge and transport power were reduced. Furthermore, sand-sluicing operations at the sites of water withdrawal returned most of the sediments to the main channel. The channel in the El Paso-Juarez Valley at the upstream end of the international boundary adjusted by reducing its width and depth. Inasmuch as channel geometry is a function of the at or near bankfull discharges that accomplish most of a river's work, it is not surprising that the channel constricted itself after the annual number of days of channel-forming discharge was reduced by 99 percent (Table VIII-2). According to a survey conducted by the International Boundary Commission, the cross-sectional area of the channel downstream of El Paso decreased by 20 to 50 percent during the period 1917-1932 (Ainsworth and Brown, 1933: 13).

In the valleys below the dam, where the River ran narrower, deeper, and faster than before, the adjacent floodplain aggraded 0.1 to 2.0 feet between 1917-1932 (Ainsworth and Brown, 1933: 4). At El Paso, where the El Paso-Juarez Valley was dependent on moderate floods with which to scour the channel bed and entrench the River, the mean channel bed elevation was raised to a level higher than that of some low-lying streets of both El Paso and Juarez. Depending on the source consulted, the net increase in elevation of the bed during the period 1907-1933 was between 9 and 12 feet (Reinhardt, 1937: 48).

Surprising at first is the fact that, during the ten year pre-dam era from 1907-1917, the channel at El Paso filled just as much as it did in the fifteen year post-dam era from 1917-1932. However, some of the pre-dam aggradation might be attributed to the River's tendency to adjust and flatten the higher gradient induced by the 1899 artificial cutoff of Cordova, and to replace bed material scoured by the great floods of 1905 and 1907. Also, sand-sluicing at the site of the International Diversion Dam drew off flow both into the United States Canal and into the Old Mexican Canal, while returning most of the sand

TABLE VIII-2

El Paso Discharge Data for 1890-1931

	1890-1913		1916-1931	
	YEAR OF LEAST DISCHARGE 1902	AVERAGE FOR PERIOD	YEAR OF MAXIMUM DISCHARGE 1905	AVERAGE FOR PERIOD
Discharge in acre-feet for year	50,759	918,327	2,014,096	637,769
Days per year with no flow 0.0 c.f.s.	158	70	0.0	0.0
Days per year with low flow 1-1000 c.f.s.	203	193	216	219.6
Days per year with mod. flow 1000-5000 c.f.s.	4	74	88	145.4
Days per year with high flow 5000 or more c.f.s.	0	28	61	0.3

Source: Ainsworth and Brown, 1933: 20.

sediment load to the channel below the dam (Ainsworth and Brown, 1933: 63-65). In reference to channel aggradation at El Paso, Ainsworth and Brown concluded that:

This characteristic, however, has been accelerated by the construction of Elephant Butte Dam. Sand scoured from the upper reaches of the river now continually accumulates in the river bed, as the river flow past El Paso has been so depleted by irrigation diversions that the power to transport the sand load downstream is largely lost (Ainsworth and Brown, 1933: 5).

Thus, it appears that the aggradation problems at El Paso resulted from the loss of discharges capable of performing sediment transport and occasional scour. More total annual sediment may have been carried through the El Paso cross-section before Elephant Butte than after, owing to greater annual and peak discharges. Therefore, the fact that the River recharged itself with sediment below the dam does not alone account for accelerated downstream aggradation in the post-dam era.

Of even greater importance in analyzing the effect of Elephant Butte on the international boundary are the lateral movements of the River. These can best be described in terms of river length. The sinuosity of the natural River, the ratio of river length to valley length, was approximately 1.2 in the valleys upstream of El Paso and 1.9 in the El Paso-Juarez Valley. In 1917 the channel length between Elephant Butte and El Paso was 149.35 miles. By 1932 the channel was reduced to 143.07 miles, a loss of 6.28 miles due largely to artificial cutoffs.

Somewhat puzzling is the disclosure in a 1931 Boundary Commission report that, in the Mesilla Valley just upstream of El Paso, the Rio Grande had at one time a channel that was much more sinuous than the channel of the early 1900's. Apparently, the older channel ran narrower and deeper than the channel of the early 1900's, and had a highly-developed meander pattern, as indicated by numerous cutoffs on the floodplain. In other words, the channel pattern in the Mesilla Valley was at one time similar to that of the El Paso-Juarez Valley (Fiock, 1931: 5). No explanation has been offered in Boundary Commission reports to account for the seemingly rapid change from a well developed meander pattern to one involving a broad, straight master channel and internal braiding. Contributing factors may have been climatic persistence (seasonal concentration of rain, drought, etc.), catastrophic floods, native occupance and fires, or the conversion of the adjacent prairies into deserts by overgrazing in the 1800's. One can speculate at best on the relative significance of a given factor, inasmuch as several factors may have operated in combination to produce the change in channel form.

Between El Paso and San Elizario in the El Paso-Juarez Valley, channel length decreased from 61.81 miles to 57.34 miles during the period 1917-1932. Now, along most major rivers in the downstream direction, discharge generally increases, gradient generally decreases, the floodplain widens, and the river becomes more sinuous. Therefore, a shortening of the Rio Grande by 4.47 miles just downstream of El Paso might intuitively be associated with decreased discharge in the post-dam era. However, the River actually shortened some 6.73 miles, all by artificial cutoffs, but added 2.26 miles by lateral erosion. Thus, 4.47 miles is the net reduction in length, although the natural tendency of the River along this reach was to lengthen. Along the channel downstream of El Paso,

> . . . there is a general tendency of the river to increase its length. Silt and sand is deposited along the inside banks on river bends and the river constantly erodes the outside bank. Thus the bends continually become sharper and more tortuous. As this process of gradual lengthening continues, the river grade becomes flatter, its ability to transport sand and silt, already poor, still further decreases, with the result that an ever increasing tendency of the river bed towards up building is manifested (Ainsworth and Brown, 1933: 32).

An even greater adjustment in length occurred in the reach of the River from San Elizario to Fort Quitman, where the average gradient is 1.5 feet per mile or less. In the twenty-five year period 1907-1932, the River's length increased from 83.00 miles to 98.48 miles, a net gain of 15.48 miles. The net gain results from 19.71 miles gained by lateral erosion and 4.23 miles lost by natural avulsions (cutoffs). Although it is not known how many of the erosion and accretion miles were added prior to damming, lengthening dominated after Elephant Butte (Ainsworth and Brown, 1933: 6-8).

Effect of Elephant Butte on Floods and Flood Capacity

As noted earlier, Elephant Butte Dam significantly reduced the variability and magnitude of flow through the valleys below. Had the main channel not adjusted itself to this regulated flow, the discharge capacity of the River and floodplain would have remained high, whereas floods themselves would practically have been eliminated. During the period 1917-1932, the ability of the channel and floodplain to conduct peak discharges was so reduced along certain reaches of the River that increasingly frequent flooding was associated with reduced discharges. These local increases in flood frequency should not suggest that Elephant Butte was ineffective or non-beneficial in terms of flood control, for the numbers of reaches along which flood frequency increased were few and the magnitudes of the floods were minimal in comparison with pre-dam figures.

The discharge capacity of the channel in the valleys directly below the dam increased as the River entrenched itself and increased its cross-sectional area. Also, the shortened channel had a steepened gradient and straightened route, producing an increase in channel efficiency. Nevertheless, the River's total efficiency probably decreased because of prolific growth of vegetation on the bars, banks, and floodplain (Ainsworth and Brown, 1933: 4,5). Tamarisk (saltcedar) is especially abundant in the southwest in riverine environments. On the Gila River, for example, the reduction in velocity of flood discharges on the floodplain on account of Tamarisk is estimated to have been largely responsible for the increment of 4 or 5 feet of sediment from a single flood (Robinson, 1958: 28). Tamarisk is plentiful in the El Paso region, and may conceivably have played an important role in helping to build the floodplain in the post-dam era.

The role of vegetation as a control of river morphology cannot be ignored in the El Paso area. Streams such as the Rio Grande that flow through arid regions and across alluvium are likely to adjust most to peak discharges by undermining their banks, widening their channel, and destroying their floodplains (Schumm, 1963: 71-88) (Chapter IV). Obviously, bank material anchored by deep-rooted vegetation will retard widening and will force the river to rise to levels that may induce flooding. As a result of the regulation of discharge by Elephant Butte Dam, the season of maximum discharge at El Paso changed from late spring to late summer and early fall. The late summer-early fall period also happens to be the season of maximum vegetative coverage along the River and its floodplain. The percent of coverage near El Paso has been estimated to double between June and September. In some years, such as 1972 where summer rains were of moderate intensity but of high frequency, plant coverage in September was probably 300 percent greater than in June (Worthington, 1972). Therefore, the changing of the season of maximum discharge at El

Paso, to coincide with the season of maximum vegetative coverage, would alone contribute toward increased flood frequencies. Downstream of El Paso, where the channel's cross-sectional area and gradient were reduced, and where the channel length and vegetative cover were increased, frequency of flooding increased after the installation of Elephant Butte Dam (Day, 1970: 64).

Rectification and Canalization

The increasingly sinuous, aggrading channel of the Rio Grande in the upper El Paso-Juarez Valley, and the attendant loss of flood protection for the sister cities, demanded a rectification program to straighten the River and to flush sediments downstream. Rectification had already been proposed in the 1890's when the International Boundary Commission organized. When the Commission was reactivated in the 1920's, the post-Elephant Butte channel problems reinforced efforts in behalf of rectification. The Commission's recommendations, contained in its Minute 129, were essentially carried out by the 1933 Treaty of Rectification (48 Stat. 1621).

FIGURE VIII-3. *Winter view of the rectified channel east of El Paso, where the Rio Grande is akin to a sewage canal. Tumbleweed accumulation in the channel enhances the already existing sedimentation problem that has reduced the width of the active channel to approximately fifty feet. Mexican levee appears on far right horizon.* (Photo by the author.)

The rectified earthen channel, completed in 1938, is about 66 feet wide and is contained by seven-foot levees spaced nearly 600 feet apart (Lawson, 1937: 457-58). It shortened the River from 155 to 88 miles between El Paso and Box Canyon just below Fort Quitman (Fig. VIII-3). The channel gradient increased from 1.8 to 3.2 feet per mile, ensuring fairly adequate flushing of sediments in the immediate El Paso area (Van Zandt, 1966: 204). Another problem discovered by the reactivated Boundary Commission of the 1920's was that of un-regulated discharge and sediment that entered the Rio Grande from several large tributary arroyos located downstream of Elephant Butte. The United States decided to construct a second dam and reservoir complex (Caballo) that would not only regulate the natural runoff and sediment, but would also regulate water releases from Elephant Butte. Caballo Dam was constructed approximately twenty-two miles downstream of Elephant Butte and began operating in 1938.

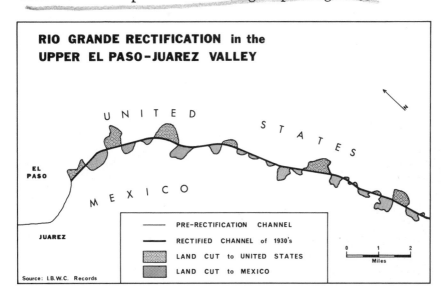

FIGURE VIII-4. *Traces of the natural and rectified channels of the Rio Grande near El Paso.*

The meander cutoffs created by channel rectification in the El Paso-Juarez Valley were eliminated in accordance with the provisions of the 1905 Banco Treaty. Cutoffs north of the channel passed to the United States; cutoffs south of the channel passed to Mexico. By the time the rectification project was completed, a total of 10,240 acres of land was exchanged, with each country receiving 5,120 acres (Fig. VIII-4). In addition, both countries secured rights-of-way on their respective sides of the Rio Grande, in order to facilitate construction and maintenance of the pilot channel. Article IV of the 1933 Treaty also provided that ". . . the permanent international boundary shall be the middle of the deepest channel . . . within such rectified river channel" (48 Stat. 1621). If a catastrophic flood should breach a levee and reroute the River, it would be the responsibility of the inundated country to repair the levee and to return the River to its permanent course.

The discharge capacity of the floodplain and rectified channel between the levees is approximately 11,000 c.f.s. Prior to Elephant Butte, the maximum peak discharge recorded at El Paso was 24,000 c.f.s. on June 12, 1905. After Elephant Butte and prior to the construction of Caballo Dam in 1938, the maximum peak discharge at El Paso was approximately 13,500 c.f.s. on September 3, 1925 (I.B.W.C. *Water Bulletin* 36, 1966: 8). Most peak discharges at El Paso since 1938 have been considerably below the design flood of 11,000 c.f.s., reflecting the effective regulation of discharge by Elephant Butte and Caballo Dams. Only once during the period 1938-1973, on September 14, 1958, was the discharge at or near the capacity of the rectified system (I.B.W.C. *Water Bulletin* 28, 1958: 7). This compares with a frequency of bankfull discharge along most natural streams of once every one or two years. As a consequence, the portions of old floodplain outside the levees have been reclaimed from the River and have experienced intensive agricultural and residential development.

Since rectification of the channel in the El Paso-Juarez Valley, the Boundary Commission has had to request appropriations for channel clearing related to vegetation and sedimentation. Most of the sediments flushed to the lower end of the rectified channel near Fort Quitman have clogged the channel and have induced the growth of Tamarisk. Annual clearance of the channel at tremendous expense is becoming a routine operation for both sections of the Boundary Commission. The United States Section alone spent $176,000 on sediment removal and control in the El Paso-Juarez Valley in 1966 (Day, 1970: 71). One author has concluded that:

The significance of alluvium and vegetation control relates to the failure of rectification architects to anticipate the necessity for continual sediment excavation and phreatophyte clearing operations to maintain the pilot channel throughout the improved reaches of the river as well as the difficulties of preserving the stream channel at the lower end of the project. This program is a costly element of project maintenance, but no indication exists in the initial joint engineering report to suggest the necessity for such measures. There is little ground for optimism that sediment and vegetation control expenses will be reduced significantly in the near future (Day, 1970: 71).

It is difficult to believe that the problem of sedimentation was not anticipated by the Boundary Commission at the time that the rectification package was designed. The Follett Report that clearly described the depositional nature of the Rio Grande in the El Paso region had been in the Commission records for more than two decades prior to the signing of the 1933 Rectification Treaty. Also, the Commission was well aware of the aggradation of the channel bed that occurred in the El Paso-Juarez Valley during the fifteen-year period after the construction of Elephant Butte. Therefore, it was basically a sedimentation problem that led to the 1933 Treaty and rectification. What the Commission likely did not know was the degree to which the sedimentation problem would persist after rectification. In recent years the United States has installed numerous small sediment control dams on tributary arroyos in southern New Mexico. These sediment control measures, all upstream from El Paso, should produce an eventual decline of sediment accumulation in the main channel of the rectified reach.

Between 1938 and 1943, the United States Section of the International Boundary Commission completed the Rio Grande Canalization Project. This project was essentially an extension of channel rectification upstream from the American Dam at El Paso, through the Mesilla Valley, to a point two miles downstream of Caballo Dam. The

United States undertook this independent action to provide flood control in southern New Mexico and to insure delivery to Mexico of the water it was granted in the 1906 Treaty (Day, 1970: 66-67). Total length of the canalized reach, excluding the 8.6-mile reach through Selden Canyon, is 105.6 miles (Vandertulip, 1974). The discharge capacity of the canalized section decreases from 22,000 c.f.s. near Caballo Dam to approximately 12,000 c.f.s. near El Paso (Baker, 1943: 3). This reduction in discharge capacity in the downstream direction reflects the large amount of water withdrawn for irrigation purposes in the agricultural valleys between Caballo and El Paso. Upon completion of canalization, government rights-of-way protected the Rio Grande from private irrigators in the reach from Caballo to Fort Quitman, save for the few miles of channel around the Chamizal and Cordova tracts.

Flood Control on the Lower Rio Grande

It is impossible to discuss discharges on the lower Rio Grande without considering the Rio Conchos that joins the River at Presidio. As mentioned earlier, the Conchos is the principal supplier of water to the lower Rio Grande, whereas the amount of water contributed by the upper Rio Grande has always been negligible.

The Conchos watershed is basically an arid region that receives most of its water supply from late summer thunderstorms. Some of the precipitation is derived from remnants of autumn hurricanes and tropical storms that move inland over Mexico. The concentration of precipitation in late summer-early fall is evident from discharge records at Ojinaga, where the Conchos joins the Rio Grande across from Presidio (Table VIII-3). Slightly over half of the annual discharge at Ojinaga is recorded in the period August-October. Four dams have been constructed on the Conchos to harness the discharge. Boquilla, by far the largest of the four, was completed in 1913 and has a reservoir capacity of 2,417,000 acre-feet. Boquilla's storage capacity is approximately 10 percent greater than that for Elephant Butte on the upper Rio Grande (I.B.W.C. records).

Just upstream from the junction of the Rio Grande and Rio Conchos, at the Upper Presidio Gaging Station, peak discharge recorded before Elephant Butte was 15,200 c.f.s. on June 12, 1912; after Elephant Butte, on August 18, 1928, the record discharge is only 6,400 c.f.s. At the Lower Presidio Gaging Station, downstream from the confluence of the two rivers, record peak discharge of 162,000 c.f.s. occurred on September 11, 1904, long before the dam building period (Table VIII-4). On the same date, the Upper Presidio Gaging Station's mean discharge was a mere 285 c.f.s.! After the building of Boquilla, the record discharge below the confluence, recorded on September 22, 1917, was still 140,000 c.f.s. (*Report on Flood Control Investigation Central Section Presidio Valley*, 1940: 18 and Table II).

TABLE VIII-3

Mean Monthly Conchos Discharge at Ojinaga

MONTH	DISCHARGE IN 1000 ACRE-FEET	MONTH	DISCHARGE IN 1000 ACRE-FEET
January	60.7	July	94.9
February	49.6	August	139.6
March	62.3	September	245.4
April	37.1	October	136.6
May	25.1	November	65.3
June	38.5	December	64.8

Source: Cravioto G., 1946: 7.

TABLE VIII-4

Presidio Maximum Flood Discharges

DATE	DISCHARGE IN C.F.S.	DATE	DISCHARGE IN C.F.S.
9-11-04	162,000	9-8-42	59,400
9-23-17	140,000	9-14-44	43,900
10-2-32	106,000	10-1-58	54,300
9-22-38	68,000	9-2-66	18,600
5-25-41	31,500	9-23-68	16,500*

Source: Friedkin, 1971: 10.

*Listed at 23,000 c.f.s. in *Floods of September*, 1968, 1969.

This figure illustrates the tremendous distance and drainage area between Boquilla and Presidio in which unregulated runoff enters the Conchos.

In September, 1968, water spilled over Boquilla Dam for the first time in twenty-six years. This spill, plus downstream tributary drainage to the Conchos, generated a peak discharge in the Presidio-Ojinaga Valley of 23,000 c.f.s. The Rio Grande channel in this valley appears to have adjusted its geometry to generally decreased discharges in the post-dam era just as the channel did in the El Paso-Juarez Valley. The peak 1968 discharge filled the underfit channel and breached the series of private levees by overtopping, seepage, etc., with losses to agriculture estimated at $559,995. At the same time, the channel in the upper Presidio Valley was practically dry (*Floods of September,* 1968, 1969: 2-6). The adjustment of the geometry of the Presidio channel to decreased discharge and increased vegetation is also illustrated by the 1958 flood of 54,300 c.f.s. that crested 0.17 foot higher than a 1932 flood with a discharge of 106,000 c.f.s. (Friedkin, 1971: 12). Plans for rectification of the channel in the Presidio Valley are discussed in Chapter X.

Farther downstream on the lower Rio Grande, problems of flood control and boundary changes were just as acute as those encountered at El Paso and Presidio. Record flood discharges on the lower Rio Grande are approximately forty to fifty times greater than those recorded in the El Paso-Juarez Valley. Peak discharges recorded from two major lower Rio Grande tributaries, the Pecos and Devils Rivers, are 948,000 c.f.s. and 597,000 c.f.s. respectively. The maximum recorded discharge anywhere on the Rio Grande occurred in 1954 at Del Rio, where 1,158,000 c.f.s. roared through the valley where the Rio Grande and Pecos waters merge. A flood in the same area in 1865 was estimated at 1,500,000 c.f.s. (Day, 1970: 17; Table VIII-5). Downstream at Eagle Pass and Laredo, this 1865 flood had estimated discharges of 1,236,000 c.f.s. and 950,000 c.f.s. respectively (Keeler, 1960: 4; Table VIII-6). The last major downstream tributary to the Rio Grande with significant discharge is the Rio San Juan from Mexico. Most of its discharge has been diverted near its mouth, but on occasion it contributes as much as 350,000 c.f.s. to the Rio Grande (Day, 1970: 14).

Prior to the 1930's, most efforts at harnessing the lower Rio Grande were conducted at the local and state level and were largely concentrated on the design of levees and interior floodways. In 1932, the International Boundary Commission suggested an international effort at flood control, which was effected by the Lower Rio Grande Flood Control Project (L.R.G.F.C.P.) of the 1930's and 1940's. Altogether, more than 300 miles of levee and floodway have been built and maintained in the United States, while in Mexico the figure approaches 150 miles (Day, 1970: 92-93; Fig. VIII-5).

TABLE VIII-5

Del Rio Maximum Flood Discharges

DATE	DISCHARGE IN C.F.S.	DATE	DISCHARGE IN C.F.S.
June, 1865	1,500,000	9-16-19	385,000
6-28-54	1,158,000	6-13-99	300,000
9-1-32	620,000	9-22-19	290,000
9-18-32	532,000	10-21-14	270,000
6-24-48	460,000	4-6-00	250,000

Source: Keeler, 1960: 8.

TABLE VIII-6

Laredo Maximum Flood Discharges

DATE	DISCHARGE IN C.F.S.	DATE	DISCHARGE IN C.F.S.
June, 1865	950,000	9-18-19	192,000
6-29-54	716,900	5-31-25	189,000
9-3-32	335,000	9-26-64	180,000
6-2-22	312,000	6-16-35	176,000
6-26-48	299,500	6-15-99	172,000

Source: Keeler, 1956; I.B.W.C. *Water Bulletin 34*, 1964.

Agreement on the allocation of lower Rio Grande waters was not reached until 1944, largely because most of the flow originates in Mexican tributaries. The Water Treaty of 1944 provided for international dams designed for flood control, irrigation, hydroelectric power, and recreation (Fig. VIII-6). Falcon Dam, a few miles above Rio Grande City, was constructed in 1953; Amistad Dam, above Del Rio, was constructed in 1968 (Table VIII-7). Anzalduas Dam, completed in 1960, is a diversion structure near Reynosa that conducts water into the interior floodways of the United States and into the irrigation canals of Mexico.

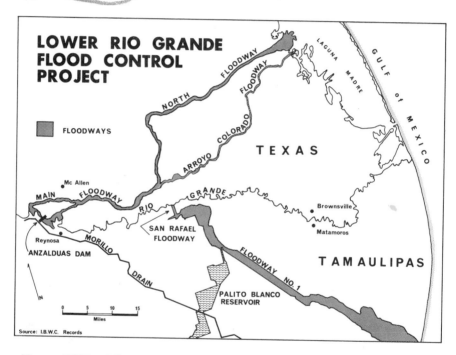

FIGURE VIII-5. *Elements of the Lower Rio Grande Flood Control Project.*

The L.R.G.F.C.P. was put to a severe test in September, 1967 when Hurricane Beulah moved up the Rio Grande Valley and stagnated over the area immediately downstream of Falcon Dam.

Intense rains of 20 to 30 inches fell in this area on September 20, 21, and 22, which resulted in the recent unprecedented flood on the lower Rio Grande. The runoff and discharge to the Rio Grande was inordinately high because the hurricane storms in September were preceded by heavy storms in August which not only saturated the watershed, but also filled the only reservoir in the basin — Mexico's Marte R. Gomez Reservoir on the Rio San Juan, which has a capacity of 760,000 acre-feet (Friedkin, 1967: 1).

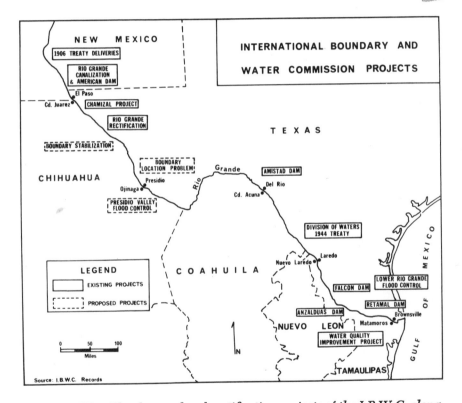

FIGURE VIII-6. *Flood control and rectification projects of the I.B.W.C. along the Rio Grande.*

Peak discharge from the storm runoff at Rio Grande City reached 210,000 c.f.s. on September 22, 1967, or approximately double the previous record discharge of 1909. This flow was also 50 percent greater than the L.R.G.F.C.P. design flood of 140,000 c.f.s. Interior floodways of the United States carried off a peak discharge of 124,000 c.f.s., 62,000 c.f.s. in both the North Floodway and the Arroyo Colorado. Another 65,000 c.f.s. was drained by the Mexican Floodway, and the remaining discharge passed through the natural channel to Browns-

TABLE VIII-7

Major Lower Rio Grande Dams

	FALCON	AMISTAD
LOCATION	75 miles downstream from Laredo	12 miles upstream from Del Rio
YEAR COMPLETED	1954	1969
MATERIAL	earthen and concrete	earthen and concrete
LENGTH	26,294 feet	32,000 feet
HEIGHT	150 feet	254 feet
FUNCTIONS	flood control, power, recreation	flood control, power, recreation
RESERVOIR CAPACITY	4,080,800 acre-feet	5,658,600 acre-feet
WATER SHARES	U.S. 58.6% Mexico 41.4%	U.S. 56.2% Mexico 43.8%
COST IN U.S. DOLLARS	U.S. 25,905,500 Mexico 20,159,500	U.S. 34,461,000 Mexico 26,560,000

Source: Texas Water Development Board, 1971: 2304.0A, 2306.0A, and I.B.W.C. Records.

ville, peaking at 16,000 c.f.s. The only serious damage from flooding occurred along the Arroyo Colorado when a diversion control structure failed at its head. Two cities and 20,000 acres of farm land were severely inundated. Yet, the overall efficiency of the L.R.G.F.C.P. is impressive when one considers that many other cities and another 400,-000 acres of farm land escaped this catastrophic event (Friedkin, 1967: 1-5). Brownsville's peak discharge of 16,000 c.f.s. was less than half the record flood of 1902 that resulted from upstream discharges

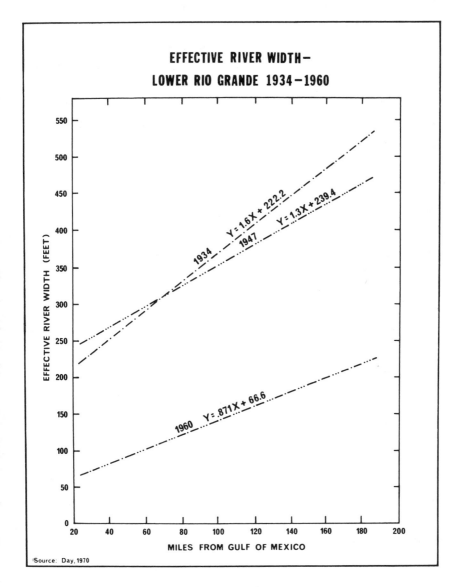

FIGURE VIII-7. *Changes in the effective channel width of the Rio Grande downstream from Falcon Dam.*

significantly lower than the discharges of 1967 (I.B.W.C. records).

A positive effect that dams and floodways are having on the boundary is reflected by the cutting of only one banco on the lower Rio Grande since the completion of Falcon. Nevertheless, there are problems induced by damming which might promote a channel and boundary shift. Since the filling of Falcon Reservoir in 1954, and the regulation of discharge, the effective channel width of the River has been significantly reduced (Fig. VIII-7, taken from Day, 1970). This reduction in channel efficiency has increased the threat of serious floods and boundary changes should the reservoir not be able to absorb maximum discharges. Part of the problem has been alleviated by the completion of Amistad and Anzalduas Dams. It remains to be seen what long-term effect on channel morphology, and hence on the boundary, the recent regulation of discharge and sediment will have.

IX

CHAMIZAL RESOLVED

ᶘᶏ After Chamizal was excluded from the 1933 Rectification Plan, the issue of jurisdiction over the tract was raised again with Presidents Truman and Eisenhower. In general, Chamizal did not receive widespread publicity again until 1962. Therefore, it is not surprising to hear the younger generation of El Pasoans who grew up in the city in the 1940's and 1950's refer to the Chamizal as "just another neighborhood" (Ingle, 1971). However, the issue arose once more in June, 1962, at a meeting in Mexico City between President Kennedy and the Mexican President Mateos. Kennedy, eager to bolster the United States image in the Organization of American States and the Alliance for Progress, came to regard the United States 1911 Award rejection as a black mark in his country's foreign relations. In July, 1963 he ". . . approved the recommendations for a complete solution to the Chamizal . . . by giving effect in today's circumstances to the 1911 international arbitration award" (*Department of State Bulletin* XLIX, 1963: 199). The circumstances referred to by Kennedy included the resettlement of 3,700 United States citizens in the affected zone and compensation of these people for land and improvements valued at approximately 20 million dollars. In August, 1963 the Chamizal Treaty was signed (15 U.S.T. 21).

Article 1 of the 1963 Treaty provided for a relocation of the River in a 4.3-mile cement-lined channel between El Paso and Juarez, on an axis determined in Minute No. 214 of the International Boundary and Water Commission. The Chamizal Channel, with a discharge capacity of 24,000 c.f.s., opened in 1968 and became a fixed reach of the international boundary (Fig. IX-1).

In order to locate the channel described in Article 1, it was necessary to determine the appropriate acreages to be transferred to either country. The Commission jointly determined the most probable location of the 1864 channel, according to the 1911 Award, and decided that the area south of the 1864 channel was 437 acres. However, the United States refused to transfer a number of areas in the northern portion of the 437-acre tract which had become highly-developed, integral portions of south El Paso. A compromise was reached whereby Mexico would receive 366 Chamizal acres, plus an additional 71 acres to be cut from the United States just east of Cordova Island (Fig. IX-2). In return, Mexico relinquished its claim to north Chamizal.

FIGURE IX-1. *Upstream view of the 1968 Chamizal Channel between Juarez on the left and El Paso on the right. Relocated irrigation canal is in right foreground.*

Each country was eager to retain the River as boundary and to have all of its territory on one side of the channel. This was impossible as long as the 396-acre Cordova tract (Mexican) remained north of the River. This tract had been of no benefit to Mexico since it was cut off in 1899. Furthermore, Cordova seriously impeded the development of south El Paso by constricting highways and railroad lines between itself and the Franklin Mountains. Simply to reroute the Rio Grande channel around Cordova would have reestablished the River as boundary, but would not have benefitted El Paso. As a consequence, the Boundary Commission included division of the Cordova tract as part of its ingenious Chamizal settlement plan. According to Article 2 of the 1963 Treaty, Mexico ceded the northern half of Cordova (193 acres) to the United States in exchange for a similar acreage cut from the United States to the east of Cordova. Therefore, the United States transferred to Mexico a 264-acre tract east of Cordova to balance the 193 acres Mexico lost from Cordova and the 71 acres Mexico relinquished in north Chamizal. As a result, the Chamizal Channel produces a smooth junction with the rectified channel of the 1930's, and the transferred areas constitute contiguous zones (Fig. IX-3). It is interesting that the Chamizal Channel is considerably longer than the natural channel. As far as is known, this is the only reach of the international Rio Grande that was lengthened, rather than shortened, by works of the Boundary Commission. Nevertheless, the smooth concrete channel is hydraulically more efficient than the shorter natural channel.

Articles 3, 4, and 6 of the 1963 Treaty essentially establish the middle of the new channel as the permanent international boundary, and insure that all rights-of-way on the north bank belong to the United States; those on the south bank belong to Mexico. Provisions were also made whereby each country secured titles to properties within its jurisdiction, before exchanges of territory were effected. Of the several parcels of land exchanged, only the Chamizal was developed. Therefore it was necessary to indemnify the United States for the transfer to Mexico of 382 structures in this zone. It was agreed that a Mexican bank would receive title to lands and structures in the Mexican Chamizal zone, in exchange for $4,676,000 paid to the United States Government.

Articles 8, 9, and 10 place on the Boundary Commission the responsibility of constructing and maintaining the Chamizal Channel, plus several bridges, with costs to be shared equally by the two countries. Article 11 states that citizenship rights of residents in the treaty zones would be unaffected by the transfers.

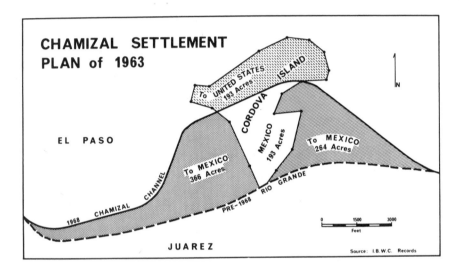

FIGURE IX-2. *Map of the Chamizal settlement zone and the relocation of the Rio Grande into a permanent boundary channel.*

The reaction of Mexico to the Chamizal settlement was enthusiastic, although she insisted that her gains had been justly awarded already in 1911. The official position of the United States Department of State is that the Chamizal settlement represents United States good faith and adherence to awards made through binding international arbitration, but in no way discredits the technical legal basis of rejection offered in 1911 (Fullerton, 1968, Vol. 1: 29). Reaction in El Paso and Texas was generally favorable, although Senator Tower questioned the right of the federal government to cede territory of one of its states without consent of that state's legislature. If one reviews other cessions made by the federal government without state approval, and if one recalls that Texas raised no objections when much larger acreages were ceded via the Banco Treaty of 1905 and the Rectification Treaty of 1933, it appears that the position of Senator Tower was not very sound. In addition, Texas was annexed to the Union in 1845 with the stipulation that the federal government has sole jurisdiction on all boundary problems with other governments (Gregory, 1963: 45).

TABLE IX-1

United States Chamizal Settlement Costs

ACTIVITY		COSTS
1. Acquisition of lands and improvements		$27,251,888.04
2. Construction		12,982,999.63
3. Engineering		1,572,675.38
4. Special benefits paid owners and tenants		919,111.18
5. Administration		616,554.34
	TOTAL COST	$43,343,228.57

Source: I.B.W.C. records.

In order to implement the Chamizal Treaty, it was necessary for the United States Government to purchase 743.54 acres of land, or slightly more than a square mile, of south El Paso. Nearly 85 percent of this area, 630.38 acres, was transferred directly to Mexico in the fall of 1967. The remaining 15 percent, 113.16 acres, was required for the Chamizal Channel, a port of entry, relocation of the Texas and Pacific, Santa Fe, and Southern Pacific Railroads, and the relocation of a principal irrigation canal. These property acquisitions alone cost the United States more than 27 million dollars (Table IX-1). Additional tens of millions have been spent in relocating public facilities of the affected zones, in constructing bridges and the Chamizal Channel, and in building an ultra-modern port of entry and customs complex at the Cordova crossing. At present, a multi-laned divided highway shuttles visitors between El Paso and the PRONAF commercial center of east Juarez via the Cordova route, crossing the Chamizal Channel and the inconspicuous dry bed of the pre-1968 Rio Grande.

FIGURE IX-3. *An aerial view of the Chamizal Zone soon after the completion of the 1968 Chamizal Channel. Note dry bed of pre-1968 Rio Grande channel.*

X

Boundary Treaty of 1970

Ｕ The Rio Conchos from Mexico joins the Rio Grande just upstream of the sister cities of Ojinaga, Chihuahua and Presidio, Texas. Here the River has a very gentle gradient and maintains a floodplain several miles wide. This is one of the most sinuous reaches of the River, with the channel length approximately three times the length of the valley. Periodic floods, usually generated on the Conchos, inundate the valley and shift the main channel across the floodplain like a contorted snake. At the time of the Emory-Salazar survey of 1852, the River was at or near the escarpment on the United States side. Today it abuts on the Mexican escarpment (Fig. X-1). During the intervening years, titles to land have become highly confused, and the Boundary Commission has not been able to award disputed tracts on the basis of the 1905 Banco Treaty. The Presidio-Ojinaga tracts constitute the last major disputed area along the United States-Mexican boundary.

In November, 1970, a Treaty with Mexico Resolving Boundary Differences was signed in Mexico City. While this treaty is specifically designed to award title and jurisdiction to the Presidio-Ojinaga tracts, it is also intended to make the River the permanent international boundary. In this respect, the 1970 Treaty is the first general boundary treaty between the two countries since 1884. Significantly, the treaty is based on recommendations of the International Boundary and Water Commission.

When the question of title to the Presidio-Ojinaga tracts first came before the Boundary Commission in 1907, Mexico claimed all of the area in dispute on the grounds that the River Valley in that area was essentially Mexican in 1852. Her claim was also based on the assumption that the River had moved by avulsion across all of the tracts. After counter arguments from the United States on the origin of the tracts and the introduction of evidence on a specific movement of the River in 1895, ". . . the Mexican Government offered to recognize 25.7 percent of the entire area as belonging to the United States." Nevertheless, the issue was not resolved by the 1907 Commission (Rogers to Nixon in Letter of Submittal, 1970 Treaty: vi).

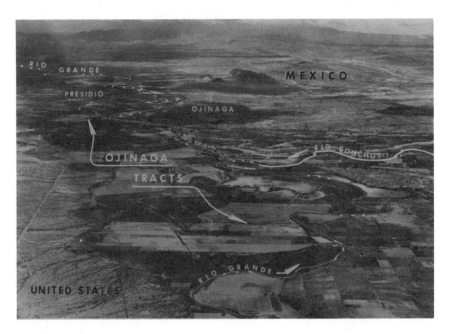

FIGURE X-1. *Downstream view of the Presidio-Ojinaga Valley and the confluence of the Rio Conchos and Rio Grande.*

Provisions of the 1970 Treaty

The United States Department of State has agreed, as part of the 1970 Treaty, to accept the 1907 Mexican offer. The acceptance is largely based on the fact that most of the Presidio Valley was Mexican at the time of original survey. While this may appear to be a concession on the part of the United States, it must be remembered that negotiations in 1907 dealt with a single boundary problem entity, whereas that entity in the 1970 Treaty becomes part of a much larger negotiation package. According to the 1970 Treaty, Mexico will be assigned 74.3% (1606.19 acres) of the disputed tracts. The assignment will be effected by rectifying the Rio Grande in the Presidio Valley ". . . so as to transfer from the north to the south side of the Rio Grande an area of 1606.19 acres (650 hectares)" (1970 Treaty, Article 1). The United States Section of the Boundary Commission anticipates completion of the rectified boundary channel and the transfer of the lands to Mexico in late 1975 (McNealy, 1974). Prior to 1970 it was not economically feasible to rectify this portion of the River, largely on account of inadequate flood control.

Article I of the 1970 Treaty also eliminates two troublesome areas south of the River which belong to the United States. In 1906, a United States firm illegally cut a new channel when the River threatened to shift its course at a meander bend. As a result, a parcel of land (419 acres) known as the Horcon tract became attached to Mexico (Fig. X-2). Since 1906, it has been impossible for the United States to exercise jurisdiction in the tract, and a Mexican village has encroached on the area. The second United States tract on the Mexican side of the River is known as Beaver Island (approximately 63 acres). It was assigned to the United States by the Boundary Commission in 1924. These two areas, almost 482 acres, pass to Mexico by the 1970 Treaty. In return, an equal acreage will be transferred from Mexico to the United States when treaty plans for rectifying the channel upstream from Hidalgo-Reynosa are put into effect.

The most difficult task undertaken by the Boundary Commission has been the awarding of islands, especially along the lower Rio Grande. These islands, numbered in hundreds, are semipermanent features at best. More often their life spans the interval between floods that occur every few weeks or months. A few larger islands persist where vegetative cover protects them against the torrential floodwaters. As of 1970, the Boundary Commission recognizes eleven United States islands (1271 acres) attached to Mexico, seven Mexican islands (323 acres) attached to the United States, and 301 islands

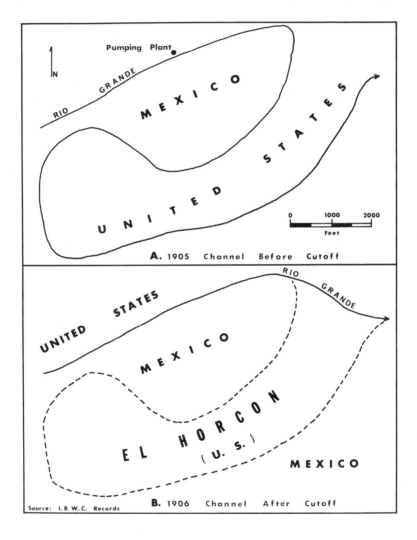

FIGURE X-2. *Formation of the Horcon Tract by an artificial cutoff.*

of indeterminant acreage assigned to neither country. Hence, the 1970 Treaty automatically assigns these islands in much the same way as banco-lands were awarded in 1905, by reestablishing the River as boundary. Islands north of the boundary channel pass to the United States; those to the south pass to Mexico. The two sections of the Boundary Commission have agreed that, when assignment of islands is complete, the United States will receive 252 fewer acres than Mexico. On this count, the 1970 Treaty stipulates that an equal acreage will be ceded by Mexico to the United States when the River is rectified downstream from Presidio. The brief attention here given to the problem of islands relates to the fact that in 1972 the two sections of the Boundary Commission were negotiating over procedures concerning the island assignment provision of the 1970 Treaty (Hamlyn, 1972). Hopefully, more information will become available within the next few years.

With the exception of rectified reaches of the River, the 1970 Treaty recognizes the natural channel as the international boundary. According to Article 2:

... the international boundary ... shall run along the middle of the channel occupied by normal flow and, ... along the middle of the channel which in normal flows has the greater or greatest average width (1970 Treaty).

This provision appears to be much more practical than those of preceding treaties. The 1884 Treaty designated as boundary the center of the normal channel, which might or might not be the deepest, widest, or fastest flowing channel (Chapter IV). In contrast, the 1905 Banco Treaty used the middle of the deepest channel to determine the boundary. Such a boundary is somewhat easier to demarcate than one which follows the normal channel, although it demands underwater measurements. The 1970 Treaty avoids the mention or use of the term *thalweg*, and designates the widest channel as boundary. This can be easily demarcated on air photos, without the necessity of expensive ground surveys and depth measurements in active channels. Article 2 also requires the Boundary Commission to remark the boundary on appropriate maps at least once every ten years.

Article 3 of the 1970 Treaty recognizes the same processes of channel change as are recognized in international law, ranging from erosion and deposition within existing channels to the severing of tracts of land by the cutting of new channels. Noteworthy in the 1970 Treaty is the avoidance of terms such as *accretion* and *avulsion*. Of tremendous significance is the fact that erosion and deposition are not restricted by the modifiers of "slow and gradual" as contained in the 1884 Treaty. Instead,

> When the Rio Grande . . . moves laterally eroding one of its banks and depositing alluvium on the opposite bank, the international boundary shall continue to follow the middle of the channel . . . which in normal flow has the greatest average width . . . (1970 Treaty, Article 3).

It is in the area of tracts severed by avulsion (the cutting of a new channel) where the 1970 Treaty departs from accepted international law. Traditionally, severed tracts are retained by the former sovereign, even if a portion of the boundary becomes dry. This rule of international law must be "violated" somewhere in the 1970 Treaty in order to be consistent with the reestablishment of a fluvial boundary in Article 2. Such is the case in the succeeding Article where the Commission is charged with physically restoring the River to its pre-avulsion channel when the newly-formed tract exceeds either 617.76 acres in area, or a population of 100 inhabitants. As an option in cases where such restoration is not feasible, the Commission must restore the acreage lost to the injured country as part of a rectification project near the site of avulsion.

Severed tracts of less than 617.76 acres and a population of less than 100 inhabitants are awarded in one of two ways. First, the injured country can restore the channel to its pre-avulsion channel within a period of three years (plus a maximum one-year extension) if it wishes to retain the tract. If restoration is not made within that period, the segregated tract passes to the new sovereign, and the new River channel becomes the international boundary. In the latter case, the former sovereign is given acreage credit by the Boundary Commission, to be granted at a later date in rectification projects, or be restored by natural movements of the River. In summary, the River is retained as boundary, regardless of its shifting course and the processes that accomplish the alteration.

Another boundary problem not previously coped with by treaty is that of the shifting mouth of the Rio Grande. The River has periodically flooded its delta, often leaving a new master channel hundreds of yards from the previous boundary channel. During the 116-year period of 1853-1969, the mouth shifted at a minimum average rate of 127 feet per year (Table X-1). In general, the River shifted 7,200 feet northward during the interval 1853-1958, and shifted 7,100 feet southward between 1958 and 1969. These figures are minima inasmuch as the latitudinal position of the mouth as shown on Boundary Commission maps is known for only eleven surveys during the 116-year period. For instance, the net shift northward of 1,550 feet during the era 1853-1897 gives no indication of what was probably an oscillatory shift that may have totaled several miles. Also, six of the eleven known positions are post-1957 and indicate an average annual shift of 650 feet for the twelve year period 1957-1969. The castastrophic nature of some of the shifts is illustrated by the fact that Hurricane Carla in 1961 forced the River to shift southward 5,425 feet in a period of only a few days.

The shifting nature of the Rio Grande's mouth is directly related to flow regimes, sedimentation rates, longshore currents, and tropical storms. During low and moderate flows, the sediment deposited near

TABLE X-1

Changes in Position of Rio Grande Mouth

INTERVAL	NET SHIFT IN FEET	DIRECTION OF SHIFT
1853-1897	1550	North
1897-1910	375	North
1910-1926	1800	North
1926-1946	1800	North
1946-1957	1300	North
1957-1958	375	North
1958-1961a	1500	South
1961a-1961b	5425	South
1961b-1967	375	South
1967-1969	200	North

Source: Compiled from unpublished maps of the I.B.W.C.

the mouth is reworked by the sea and redistributed across the mouth in the form of a bar built by north-flowing longshore currents. This bar builds out from the south bank and continually forces the mouth northward (Fig. X-3). As the River shifts northward along the coast, its gradient lessens in response to the increase in length, and its ability to transport its load diminishes. The highest known latitude reached by the mouth was recorded in 1958, when the River ran parallel to the coast for more than a mile before reaching the Gulf, and the mouth was clogged with large island-like bars. Three years later, in 1961, Hurricane Carla battered the River's mouth, while its accompanying floodwaters on the delta forced the River to shift southward and take a more direct (easterly) route to the sea. This avulsive change brought the mouth of the Rio Grande back to its approximate 1853 position. There is no reason to believe that, in the absence of tropical storms and large delta floods, the River will not again shift northward (Hamlyn, 1972).

According to the Banco Treaty, the international boundary occupied the middle of the deepest active channel and extended several miles into the Gulf of Mexico. Thus, the shifting of the mouth and the maritime boundary has at times turned the delta region into a jurisdictional no-man's-land. Just as important, rights to offshore mineral and marine resources have become obscured. According to the 1970 Treaty, a permanent maritime boundary of twelve nautical miles, fixed by latitude and longitude, will extend seaward from a point approximately 2,000 feet offshore (Fig. X-4). The inshore point will serve as a pivot from which a straight line will be drawn to "the center of the mouth of the Rio Grande, wherever it may be located . . ." (1970 Treaty, Article 5). That portion of the near-shore zone that changes jurisdiction in the future will be dependent not only on the frequency and magnitude of natural events, but also on the effectiveness of the Lower Rio Grande Flood Control Project.

Provisions are also made in the 1970 Treaty for the government acquisition of lands to be transferred or be used for rights-of-way. Obviously, citizens who find their lands being transferred must be compensated. Compensation is to be paid by the country which loses territory, on the assumption that the same country will gain revenue from the sale of lands it receives elsewhere. The 1970 Treaty also charges the Boundary Commission with excavation, rectification, and clearing of channels, as well as with relocating bridge monument markers after the boundary channel has shifted. Total cost to the United States to effect the treaty will be in excess of 10 million dollars (Table X-2). Finally, the 1970 Treaty terminates entirely the Treaties of 1884 and 1905, plus specific articles of the Treaties of 1848, 1853, 1889, and 1933 which are inconsistent with the 1970 Boundary Treaty.

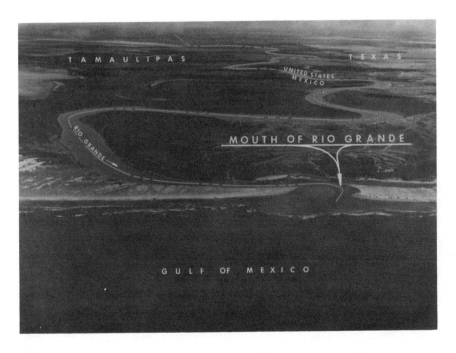

FIGURE X-3. *View of the Rio Grande's mouth in 1965. Longshore currents built the young bar that is growing across the mouth and forcing the River northward.*

Problems and Prospects

Much like the Treaties of 1905, 1933, and 1963, which appeared to

---

TABLE X-2

Projected United States 1970 Treaty Costs

PROJECT	COST (U.S. DOLLARS)
1. Land acquisition and relocation of channel in the Presidio-Ojinaga Valley	$ 3,800,000
2. Rectification of channel above Presidio-Ojinaga Valley	2,000,000
3. Relocation of channel below Presidio-Ojinaga	1,500,000
4. Land acquisition and relocation of channel on lower Rio Grande near Hidalgo-Reynosa	1,500,000
5. Easements on north bank	1,300,000
6. Survey and mapping	268,000
TOTAL	$10,368,000

Source: International Boundary and Water Commission Records.

---

solve the problems of their day, the 1970 Treaty appears to be very practical from a legal, political, and engineering standpoint. Nevertheless, several potential problems might arise both because of and in spite of the treaty. The severity of these problems and their solution will determine whether or not this is ". . . a treaty to end all treaties between the U.S. and Mexico" (El Paso *Herald-Post*: December 28, 1971).

Of special concern is the subjective portion of Article 3, whereby normal flow will determine the boundary. Normal flow has no quantitative limits of discharge, and hence must be determined for every reach of the River along which boundary questions arise. According to the United States Section of the International Boundary and Water Commission:

The Treaty does not define normal flow except to say that normal flows shall exclude flood flows, but says that they shall be determined by the Commission in each case. Therefore, an exact method, applicable in all cases, cannot be defined, since it may vary with the location, available records, and even with the engineers making the determination.

The normal channel, referred to in the 1884 Treaty in describing the boundary, has been taken to mean the channel occupied by normal flow, which is considered to be the average of all flows, with the existing state of stream development, excluding unusual floods and droughts. Flood flows may be defined as those that exceed the channel capacity, or those that cause appreciable damages, which may vary with time and locality on a stream. Also, it would not be proper to include in the average an infrequent period of little or no flow in a stream which generally flows several hundred c.f.s. Therefore, some judgment will have to be used by the Commission in each case of joint determination of "normal flow" (Hamlyn, 1971).

While one can admire the optimism of the Commission about being able to agree on normal flows, one must question how successful that agency will be should future relations between the two governments and between the two boundary Sections become less amicable than they are at present. Therefore, it is hoped that the Commission will establish a workable procedure for determining normal flows and that such a procedure will be adopted and become binding in the form of a Commission Minute.

Another potential problem is the discharge capacity of the boundary channel and levee system proposed for the Presidio Valley. Current plans call for an earthen boundary channel with an estimated bankfull discharge of 10,000 c.f.s., which is approximately the same capacity as that of the existing channel. Levees will add another 32,000 c.f.s. to the system's discharge capacity, if 4 feet of freeboard is retained to prevent overtopping and seepage. Therefore, the rectified system's total design flood is of the order of 42,000 c.f.s., which in the Presidio Valley has a recurrence interval of once every twenty-five years (Friedkin, 1971: 14). In reality, the 4 feet of freeboard will likely increase the system's capacity to something on the order of a fifty-year flood. If one considers the tremendous floods which have ravaged the Presidio Valley downstream of the Rio Conchos-Rio Grande confluence, it appears that the capacity of the proposed system is at best moderate. Just two years before the signing of the 1970 Treaty, peak discharge in a Presidio Valley flood was measured at 23,000 c.f.s., or more than double the discharge capacity of the proposed channel

(Chapter VIII). However, the seemingly low to moderate design flood is the most that can be economically justified for the predominantly agricultural Presidio Valley. Also, the design capacity of the proposed system becomes less alarming if confidence is placed in the major dams and reservoirs along the two rivers upstream of the Presidio Valley. The recent dam building projects on the Rio Conchos suggest that the Commission's confidence in the Presidio Channel has some justification, although the possibility remains of major flooding after a catastrophic natural event.

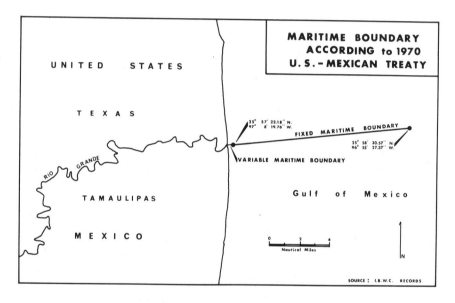

FIGURE X-4. *Proposed maritime boundary as described in 1970 Treaty.*

The length of the proposed Presidio Channel between the end points of rectification is 9.79 miles, or 6.16 miles less than the natural channel. As a result, the channel gradient will increase from approximately 2.80 feet per mile to 4.48 feet per mile. This raises the question of whether the increased gradient and increased velocity will contribute to degradation or to aggradation below the rectified reach. According to the United States Section of the Boundary Commission, "Preliminary studies indicate that the effect, if any, will probably be minor aggradation" (Hamlyn, 1971). Such aggradation would necessitate periodic channel clearing and sediment removal similar to that undertaken in the lower end of the rectified El Paso-Juarez Valley. What effect this would have on the Commission's appropriations request and budget is not known.

While corrective measures solve immediate problems and needs, no guarantee exists that these measures will not induce other severe problems at a later date. This fact was demonstrated by the installation of Elephant Butte and the ensuing aggradation in the El Paso-Juarez Valley that produced an increasingly sinuous channel and decreased flood protection (Chapter VIII). During the first half of this century, the effects of Boundary Commission projects on channel behavior were at best only generally known and not predictable in a definitive sense.

More recently, studies in fluvial geomorphology have quantified certain aspects of river behavior. Specifically, it can be demonstrated by formula that rivers which flow through unconsolidated material, such as alluvium, will adjust their hydraulic geometry (width, depth, and velocity) quite rapidly in response to variable discharges (Leopold, Wolman, and Miller, 1964: 215-219). In addition to this tendency for an equilibrium of width, depth, and velocity, streams also strive toward an equilibrium of length. Equilibrium of length is implied by the fact that velocity is primarily a depth-slope product, and that an equilibrium of velocity must necessarily be maintained by an equilibrium of gradient, other factors remaining constant. The straightest path (shortest length) taken by a river usually occurs during flood discharges when a highly efficient channel is needed to conduct the flow.

Obviously, straightening of a channel, either by rectification or by natural meander cutoffs, results in locally increased gradients and increased channel efficiency. Subsequently, the river adjusts to the local disequilibrium in gradient by sedimentation and backfilling below the over-steepened reach, or possibly by reinitiating lateral cutting to reduce the gradient and to replace the length lost by straightening. The work of several governmental agencies, especially the Army Corps of Engineers, has shown that straightening of a channel in one reach usually leads to an increase in sedimentation and the resumption of meandering in a downstream reach. Also, there is a long-term tendency for the rectified or straightened reach to resume its lateral cutting and meandering unless measures are taken to reinforce banks (Friedkin, 1945).

Equilibrium length is also implied in the concept of the graded river, whose longitudinal profile is generally a smooth, concave upward curve. If no tendency for equilibrium length existed, then it is likely that the longitudinal profile would be characterized by an irregular and step-like sequence of segments, instead of the smooth curve that most alluvial rivers are known to possess. In other words, the tendency of rivers like the Rio Grande to replace miles lost by avulsion with miles created by accretion is the rule rather than the exception.

Between Rio Grande City and the Gulf of Mexico, the River is approximately twice as long (250 miles) as its valley. It has a very distinct meandering pattern that is subject to avulsive changes during flood times. An early study indicated that some sixty meander bends were severed avulsively between 1852 and 1898, shortening the River by 125 miles, or just half its natural length (Follett, 1911: 3). Yet, it is remarkable that the Boundary Commission found the River's length in 1898 to be approximately 250 miles, the same as in 1852. One can only conclude that lengthening by lateral erosion replaced the length lost by avulsion, and hence, that the lower Rio Grande has at least a quasi-equilibrium length. The processes of avulsion and accretion that lead to an equilibrium length are probably active in most alluvial systems, and although Mark Twain knew better, he was prompted to state that:

In the space of one hundred and seventy-six years, the Lower Mississippi has shortened itself two hundred and forty-two miles. That is a trifle of over one mile and a third per year. Therefore, any calm person, who is not blind or idiotic can see that . . . just a million years ago next November the Lower Mississippi River was upward of one million three hundred thousand miles long, and stuck out over the Gulf of Mexico like a fishing rod. And by the same token any person can see that seven hundred and forty-two years from now the Lower Mississippi River will be only a mile and three quarters long. . . . There is something fascinating about science. One gets such wholesale returns of conjecture out of such a trifling investment of fact (Twain, 1883: 208).

The concept of equilibrium length leads one to the inevitable question of what will happen to the Rio Grande's length downstream from those alluvial reaches which have been, or will be, rectified and shortened. The question might be answered by looking at the changes in the channel length that have occurred in the Presidio Valley following rectification of the El Paso-Juarez Valley farther upstream in the 1930's. According to the Boundary Commission, the Presidio channel was mapped at 12.70 miles long in 1895 by the United States Geological Survey. Today, the same channel is 15.94 miles long, or nearly 26 percent longer than in 1895 (Hamlyn, 1971). Although most of the increase in length can be attributed to the reduction in the number of banco-forming discharges after the building of Boquilla and Elephant Butte, it is reasonable to suspect that flushing of sediments through the canyons between Fort Quitman and Presidio since the 1930's has aided the process of aggradation and lengthening. According to records maintained for the Upper Presidio Gaging Station, aggradation has elevated the bed of the Rio Grande by approximately 6 feet during the period 1932-1970 (Henderson, 1974). Other evidence indicates that total depth of aggradation in the upper Presidio Valley since 1942 may be as much as 10 feet (McNealy, 1974). An unanswered question is, What effect will rectification in the Presidio Valley have on sediment transport through the canyons of the Big Bend region and subsequent aggradation in the reservoirs and channel of the alluvial lower Rio Grande?

With the number of provisions and built-in options contained in the 1970 Treaty, the maximum injury suffered by a country as a result of channel shifts is definitely less than that provided by any of the previous treaties. In fact, loss of large parcels of valuable land can only occur if the injured country fails to take the appropriate steps to have the channel restored to its previous course. Also, the restoration options, coupled with the ever increasing regulation of discharge, will hopefully give the trace of the Rio Grande on maps a degree of permanence not previously possessed. The 1970 Treaty has been ratified by the Senates of both countries, and project appropriations have been made. Considering the benefits it offers both countries, one can only hope the treaty is effected as soon as possible.

XI

Summary and Conclusions

🌺 It is possible to divide the history of the Rio Grande portion of the international boundary into five distinct eras. Era one is the pre-boundary or pre-1848 history of the Rio Grande, beginning about 1800. During this time the colonial giants rearranged powers, exchanged or ceded territory in North America, and alerted Mexico to the fact that it must establish a northern boundary. With the westward expansion of the United States and the settlement of interior Texas by Anglos, the pressures on Mexico multiplied. Because of the emphasis placed on the Rio Grande by explorers, colonial powers, and independent Texas in 1836, it was inevitable that Mexico would capitulate as she did at Guadalupe-Hidalgo in 1848. Neither the United States nor Mexico realized in 1848 that their boundary river would prove to be grand only in its length, variable discharge, value of water and irrigable lands, disastrous floods, shifting channels, and attendant international confrontations.

The next era ranges from 1848 to 1884, during which time the boundary was governed by the Treaties of 1848 and 1853. This could also be called the Fixed-Line Era, although United States Attorney General Cushing in 1856 opinioned that the boundary was mobile in accordance with "erosion versus avulsion" of international law. Yet, the Treaty of 1848 mentions a ". . . boundary line with due precision . . . in which . . . no change shall ever be made . . ." (9 Stat. 922).

Era three spans 1884-1905 and could appropriately be called the Highly-Variable Line Era. During this period Cushing's opinion was effected by a treaty which proved to be the least workable boundary treaty ever between the United States and Mexico. The River eroded rapidly in some reaches and carried the boundary with it; in other reaches the River avulsively severed its meanders, leaving the boundary dry and distant from the new channel. By 1890 there were

stretches along the lower Rio Grande where the boundary was actually two and three times longer than the River! Eventually an International Boundary Commission had to be assembled in order to re-
establish the boundary. Fortunately the commissioners and their engineers soon recognized that the Rio Grande could not be governed
by an international law originally designed for boundary rivers in
more humid regions where, compared to the subhumid regions, discharges are more uniform and bank stability is enhanced by greater
clay content and vegetation density.

From 1905 to 1970, the River has been governed by treaties based
on recommendations of the Boundary Commission. This period can
also be called the Mildly-Variable Line Era, for it has been regulated
by the Banco Treaty of 1905 that has successfully kept the boundary
fluvial, save for special cases such as Chamizal. It is also during this
period that increased regulation of discharge by several large dams
and reservoirs has considerably tamed the flow of the Rio Grande,
although at the same time problems of sedimentation and lengthening of the channel have arisen.

The last era, which will begin as soon as the 1970 Treaty is effected,
can be called the Highly-Restricted Variable Line Era. Rectified efficient channels, reduction of total discharge owing to increased urban
and agricultural water consumption from reservoirs, and a reduced
range of discharge due to reservoir storage, should restrict future
channel shifts in number and magnitude. Add to these factors the
treaty provisions for restoring a channel to its boundary course after
a shift, and little doubt exists that the Rio Grande as a boundary will
become fixed in the succeeding decades.

Conclusions on the River and the Law

For more than a century now, it has been the general rule of nations
to define their fluvial boundaries in terms of thalweg and to adjust
such boundaries to the subsequent channel changes wrought by the
processes of accretion and avulsion. These concepts of delineation
and regulation were given impetus in North America by the 1856
opinion of the United States Attorney General, whose advice was
sought concerning channel shifts along the international Rio Grande.

His opinion, based on court decisions and existing treaty provisions elsewhere in North America and Europe, recognized one set of rules for all rivers in reference to channel and boundary changes. Obviously, such blanket coverage is based on the assumption that all rivers behave in a similar manner.

Some rivers of subhumid zones, such as the Rio Grande, behave far differently from their humid region counterparts and demand special regulation. Much of the difference in behavior can be attributed to contrasts in climate, weathering products, vegetation types and density, and flow regimes. Along much of the Rio Grande, sparse rainfall and scant vegetation inhibit the formation of the clay end products of chemical weathering. Low amounts of clay in the soil and the minimal anchoring effect of sparse vegetation produce very friable river banks that offer little resistance to the highly variable discharges that characterize the Rio Grande and other rivers of subhumid zones. These rivers tend to be very broad, very shallow, and sometimes possess a braided, anastomotic channel pattern. Therefore, it seems impractical, if not impossible, to trace in these rivers the thalweg of international law as the boundary. In this day of aerial photography, the most practical procedure is to map the boundary from photographs, using the middle of the widest channel as boundary. This latter procedure, described in the 1970 Treaty, will be used in the future by the Boundary Commission to determine the fluvial boundary between the United States and Mexico.

Another major difference between rivers of humid and subhumid regions is in the rate at which the processes of accretion and avulsion operate. The sturdy, anchored banks of humid zones lend themselves to the development and maintenance of meanders, as well as to the cutoff of meanders by water forced out of the old channel during high discharges. In subhumid areas, overbank flooding during high discharges may be rare, owing to the ability of channels to adjust their widths. Rapid erosion within existing channels was illustrated in the cases of Chamizal and several of the bancos, where water confined to the channel produced changes in the River's position that would rival true cutoffs or avulsions in many other streams. Therefore, the laws that apply to boundary channels should consider that, along some rivers at least, major channel shifts associated with rapid erosion are the rule and cutoff by overbank flow may be the exception.

For the Rio Grande, there is a marked interrelationship between the effect of laws on the River and the effect of the River on the laws. For example, the Treaty of 1884 produced an increasingly sinuous, partially-dry boundary and negated a simple settlement of the Chamizal dispute. These situations, in turn, gave impetus to the 1905 Banco Treaty that reestablished the River as boundary, and to the 1963 Chamizal Convention that determined the boundary between El Paso and Juarez.

Problems of water rights and flooding in the El Paso-Juarez Valley were to be resolved by the 1906 Water Allocation Treaty that authorized the building of Elephant Butte Dam and Reservoir in 1916. In response to the dam and vastly altered flow regimes, the River made great adjustments in its hydraulic geometry to the point where flooding and flood potential along certain reaches were increased through channel constriction, channel lengthening, and increased sedimentation. These channel problems then led to the building of Caballo Dam and Reservoir, which further decreased channel efficiency downstream.

The poor condition of the channel in the El Paso-Juarez Valley prompted the 1933 Treaty of Rectification. Rectification was followed by canalization of the River upstream from El Paso to Caballo Dam. Rectification and canalization, in turn, led to the increased sedimentation in the lower end of the El Paso-Juarez Valley that to this day requires annual removal of silt and sand by Boundary Commission employees. Also, the net loss of water through the Canyon reach that results from increased irrigation upstream has reduced the volume of water entering the Presidio Valley, and has enhanced problems of sedimentation and channel efficiency there. The effect of Boquilla Dam, built on the Conchos in 1913, has also been disastrous in terms of decreased channel efficiency in the Presidio Valley and along the lower Rio Grande.

The Water Treaty of 1944 authorized dams on the lower Rio Grande and led to the building of Falcon and Amistad. Their effect has been to decrease channel efficiency downstream and to enhance deposition and shifting of the channel at the mouth. The combined effect of all dams regulating the Rio Grande has contributed to the need for the 1970 Treaty, which calls for rectification in the Presidio Valley and the establishment of a permanent maritime boundary.

In summary, the laws applied to the Rio Grande from 1848 to 1905 essentially complied with the accepted international law of fluvial boundaries. From 1905 to 1970, the treaties that governed the Rio Grande boundary circumvented conventional international law so that a fluvial boundary could be maintained despite the wanderings of the River. Somewhat different is the 1970 Treaty that not only retains a fluvial boundary, but also has options to restore the channel to a pre-avulsive position. Time will judge the effectiveness of the 1970 Treaty in solving, rather than generating, boundary problems.

No one knows the total cost of the effort to establish and maintain the Rio Grande as a boundary during the past 125 years. The settlement of the Chamizal case in the 1960's alone cost the United States more than 43 million dollars. Certainly these efforts and expenses have proved worthy in terms of flood control, reclamation of irrigable land, urban development, establishing jurisdictional status, etc. However, from all this gain must be subtracted the loss of aesthetic appeal. It is difficult to comprehend that the Restless River, once teeming with fish and bordered by the cottonwood oases so vividly described by explorers and settlers, has been transformed in some places into nothing more than an open sewage canal. Admittedly, such unpleasant places along the River are few and measures are being taken to clean them up.

APPENDIX

Excerpts of United States-Mexican Treaties Pertinent in Establishing or Maintaining the Rio Grande International Boundary.

I

TREATY OF PEACE, FRIENDSHIP, LIMITS, AND SETTLEMENT BETWEEN THE
UNITED STATES OF AMERICA AND THE MEXICAN REPUBLIC

Concluded at Guadalupe Hidalgo February 2, 1848; ratified by the President of the United States March 16, 1848; ratifications exchanged May 30, 1848; proclaimed by the President of the United States July 4, 1848.

ARTICLE 5

The boundary line between the two republics shall commence in the Gulf of Mexico, three leagues from land, opposite the mouth of the Rio Grande, otherwise called Rio Bravo del Norte, or opposite the mouth of its deepest branch, if it should have more than one branch emptying directly into the sea; from thence, up the middle of that river, following the deepest channel, where it has more than one to the point where it strikes the southern boundary of New Mexico; thence, westwardly along the whole southern boundary of New Mexico (which runs north of the town called Paso) to its western termination; thence, northward, along the western line of New Mexico, until it intersects the first branch of the river Gila; (or if it should not intersect any branch of that river, then, to the point on the said line nearest to such branch, and thence in a direct line to the same;) thence down the middle of the said branch and of the said river, until it empties into the Rio Colorado; thence across the Rio Colorado, following the division line between Upper and Lower California, to the Pacific Ocean.

The southern and western limits of New Mexico, mentioned in this article, are those laid down in the map, entitled "Map of the United Mexican States, as organized and defined by various acts of the Congress of said republic, and constructed according to the best authorities. Revised edition. Published at New York, in 1847, by J. Disturnell"; of which map a copy is added to this treaty, bearing the signatures and seals of the undersigned plenipotentiaries. And, in order to preclude all difficulty in tracing upon the ground the limit separating Upper from Lower California, it is agreed that the said limit shall consist of a straight line, drawn from the middle of the Rio Gila, where it unites with the Colorado, to a point on the coast of the Pacific Ocean, distant one marine league due south of the southernmost point of the port of San Diego, according to the plan of said port, made in the year 1782, by Don Juan Pantoja, second sailing master of the Spanish fleet, and published at Madrid in the year 1802, in the atlas to the voyage of the schooners *Sutil* and *Mexicana;* of which plan a copy is hereunto added, signed and sealed by the respective plenipotentiaries.

In order to designate the boundary line with due precision, upon authoritative maps, and to establish upon the ground landmarks which shall show the limits of both republics, as described in the present article, the two Governments shall each appoint a commissioner and a surveyor, who, before the expiration of one year from the date of the exchange of ratifications of this treaty, shall meet at the port of San Diego, and proceed to run and mark the said boundary in its whole course to the mouth of the Rio Bravo del Norte. They shall keep journals and make out plans of their operations; and the result, agreed upon by them, shall be deemed a part of this treaty, and shall have the same force as if it were inserted therein. The two Governments will amicably agree regarding what may be necessary to these persons, and also as to their respective escorts, should such be necessary.

The boundary line established by this article shall be religiously respected by each of the two republics, and no change shall ever be made therein, except by the express and free consent of both nations, lawfully given by the General Government of each, in conformity with its own constitution.

II

TREATY BETWEEN THE UNITED STATES OF AMERICA AND THE MEXICAN REPUBLIC RELATIVE TO THE BOUNDARY LINE, THE TRANSIT OF PERSONS ACROSS THE ISTHMUS OF TEHUANTEPEC, ETC. (GADSDEN TREATY)

Concluded at the City of Mexico December 30, 1853; ratified by the President of the United States June 29, 1854; ratifications exchanged at Washington June 30, 1854; proclaimed June 30, 1854.

ARTICLE 1

The Mexican Republic agrees to designate the following as her true limits with the United States for the future, retaining the same dividing line between the two Californias, as already defined and established according to the 5th article of the treaty of Guadalupe Hidalgo, the limits between the two republics shall be as follows: Beginning in the Gulf of Mexico, three leagues from land, opposite the mouth of the Rio Grande as provided in the fifth article of the treaty of Guadalupe Hidalgo, thence as defined in the said article, up the middle of that river to the point where the parallel of 31 deg. 47 min. north latitude crosses the same, thence due west one hundred miles, thence south to the parallel of 31 deg. 20 min. north latitude, thence along the said parallel of 31 deg. 20 min. to the 111th meridian of longitude west of Greenwich, thence in a straight line to a point on the Colorado River twenty English miles below the junction of the Gila and Colorado Rivers, thence up the middle of the said river Colorado until it intersects the present line between the United States and Mexico.

For the performance of this portion of the treaty, each of the two Governments shall nominate one commissioner, to the end that, by common consent, the two thus nominated having met in the city of Paso del Norte, three months after the exchange of the ratifications of this treaty may proceed to survey and mark out upon the land the dividing line stipulated by this article, where it shall not have already been surveyed and established by the mixed commission, according to the treaty of Guadaulpe keeping a journal and making proper plans of their operations. For this purpose if they should judge it necessary the contracting parties shall be at liberty each to unite to its respective commissioner scientific or other assistants, such as astronomers and surveyors whose concurrence shall not be considered necessary for the settlement and ratification of a true line of division between the two republics; that line shall be alone established upon which the commissioners may fix, their consent in this particular being considered decisive and an integral part of this treaty, without necessity of ulterior ratification or approval, and without room for interpretation of any kind by either of the parties contracting.

The dividing line thus established shall in all time be faithfully respected by the two Governments without any variation therein, unless of the express and free consent of the two, given in conformity to the principles of the law of nations, and in accordance with the constitution of each country respectively.

In consequence, the stipulation in the 5th article of the treaty of Guadalupe upon the boundary line therein described is no longer of any force, wherein it may conflict with that here established, the said line being considered annulled and abolished wherever it may not coincide with the present, and in the same manner remaining in full force where in accordance with the same.

ARTICLE 4

The several provisions, stipulations and restrictions contained in the 7th article of the treaty of Guadalupe Hidalgo, shall remain in force only so far as regards the Rio Bravo del Norte below the initial of the said boundary provided in the first article of this treaty that is to say below the intersection of the 31 deg. 47 min. 30 sec. parallel of latitude with the boundary line established by the late treaty dividing said river from its mouth upwards according to the 5th article of the treaty of Guadalupe.

III

CONVENTION BETWEEN THE UNITED STATES OF AMERICA AND THE UNITED
STATES OF MEXICO, PROVIDING FOR AN INTERNATIONAL BOUNDARY SURVEY
TO RELOCATE THE EXISTING FRONTIER LINE BETWEEN THE TWO COUNTRIES
WEST OF THE RIO GRANDE. (BOUNDARY CONVENTION OF 1882)

*Concluded July 29, 1882; ratification advised by the Senate August 8, 1882;
ratified by the President January 29, 1883; ratifications exchanged March
3, 1883; proclaimed March 5, 1883.*

ARTICLE 1

With the object of ascertaining the present condition of the monuments
marking the boundary line between the United States of America and the
United States of Mexico, established by the treaties of February 2, 1848,
and December 30, 1853, and for determining generally what monuments,
if any, have been destroyed or removed and may require to be rebuilt or
replaced, a preliminary reconnaissance of the frontier line shall be made
by each Government, within six months from the exchange of ratifications
of this convention. These reconnissances shall be made by parties under
the control of officers of the regular army of the respective countries, and
shall be effected in concert, in such manner as shall be agreed upon by the
commanders of the respective parties. The expense of each reconnoitering
party shall be borne by the government in whose behalf it operates.

These reconnaissance parties shall report to their respective governments, within eight months from the exchange of the ratifications of this
convention: (a) The condition of the present boundary monuments; (b)
The number of destroyed or displaced monuments; (c) The places, settled
or capable of eventual settlement, where it may be advisable to set the
monuments closer together along the line than at present; (d) The character of the new monuments required, whether of stone or iron; and their
number, approximately, in each case.

ARTICLE 2

Pending the conclusion of the preliminary reconnaissances provided in
Article 1, each government shall appoint a surveying party, consisting of
an engineering chief, two associates one of whom shall be a practical astronomer, and such number of assistant engineers and associates as it may
deem proper. The two parties so appointed shall meet at El Paso del Norte,
or at any other convenient place to be agreed upon, within six months from
the exchange of the ratifications hereof, and shall form, when combined, an
"International Boundary Commission."

ARTICLE 3

The International Boundary Commission shall be required and have the power and authority to set in their proper places along the boundary line between the United States and Mexico, from the Pacific Ocean to the Rio Grande, the monuments heretofore placed there under existing treaties whenever such monuments shall have become displaced; to erect new monuments on the site of former monuments when these shall have been destroyed; and to set new monuments at such points as may be necessary and be chosen by joint accord between the two Commissioner Engineers in Chief. In rebuilding and replacing the old monuments and in providing for new ones, the respective reports of the reconnaissance parties provided by Article 1 may be consulted; provided however that the distance between two consecutive monuments shall never exceed eight thousand meters, and that this limit may be reduced on those parts of the line which are inhabited or capable of habitation.

IV

CONVENTION BETWEEN THE UNITED STATES OF AMERICA AND THE UNITED STATES OF MEXICO, TOUCHING THE INTERNATIONAL BOUNDARY LINE WHERE IT FOLLOWS THE BED OF THE RIO GRANDE AND THE RIO COLORADO.

Concluded at Washington November 12, 1884; ratification advised by the Senate June 23, 1886; ratified by the President of the United States July 10, 1886; ratifications exchanged at Washington September 13, 1886; proclaimed September 14, 1886.

ARTICLE 1

The dividing line shall forever be that described in the aforesaid treaty and follow the center of the normal channel of the rivers named, notwithstanding any alterations in the banks or in the course of those rivers, provided that such alterations be effected by natural causes through the slow and gradual erosion and deposit of alluvium and not by the abandonment of an existing river bed and the opening of a new one.

ARTICLE 2

Any other change, wrought by the force of the current, whether by the cutting of a new bed, or when there is more than one channel by the deepening of another channel than that which marked the boundary at the time of the survey made under the aforesaid treaty, shall produce no change in the dividing line as fixed by the surveys of the International Boundary Commissions in 1852; but the line then fixed shall continue to follow the middle of the original channel bed, even though this should become wholly dry or be obstructed by deposits.

ARTICLE 3

No artificial change in the navigable course of the river, by building jetties, piers, or obstructions which may tend to deflect the current or produce deposits of alluvium, or by dredging to deepen another than the original channel under the treaty when there is more than one channel, or by cutting waterways to shorten the navigable distance, shall be permitted to affect or alter the dividing line as determined by the aforesaid commissions of 1852 or as determined by Article 1 hereof and under the reservation therein contained; but the protection of the banks on either side from erosion by revetments of stone or other material not unduly projecting into the current of the river shall not be deemed an artificial change.

V

CONVENTION BETWEEN THE UNITED STATES OF AMERICA AND THE UNITED STATES OF MEXICO TO FACILITATE THE CARRYING OUT OF THE PRINCIPLES CONTAINED IN THE TREATY OF NOVEMBER 12, 1884, AND TO AVOID THE DIFFICULTIES OCCASIONED BY REASON OF THE CHANGES WHICH TAKE PLACE IN THE BED OF THE RIO GRANDE AND THE COLORADO RIVER.

Signed at Washington March 1, 1889; ratification advised May 7, 1890; ratified by the President of the United States December 6, 1890; ratifications exchanged December 24, 1890; proclaimed December 26, 1890.

ARTICLE 1

All differences or questions that may arise on that portion of the frontier between the United States of America and the United States of Mexico where the Rio Grande and the Colorado Rivers form the boundary line, whether such differences or questions grow out of alterations or changes in the bed of the aforesaid Rio Grande and that of the aforesaid Colorado River, or of works that may be constructed in said rivers, or of any other cause affecting the boundary line, shall be submitted for examination and decision to an International Boundary Commission, which shall have exclusive jurisdiction in the case of said differences or questions.

ARTICLE 2

The International Boundary Commission shall be composed of a commissioner appointed by the President of the United States of America, and of another appointed by the President of the United States of Mexico, in accordance with the constitutional provisions of each country, of a consulting engineer, appointed in the same manner by each Government, and of such secretaries and interpreters as either Government may see fit to add to its commission. Each Government separately shall fix the salaries and emoluments of the members of its commission.

ARTICLE 3

The International Boundary Commission shall not transact any business unless both commissioners are present. It shall sit on the frontier of the two contracting countries, and shall establish itself at such places as it may determine upon; it shall, however, repair to places at which any of the difficulties or questions mentioned in this convention may arise, as soon as it shall have been duly notified thereof.

ARTICLE 4

When, owing to natural causes, any change shall take place in the bed of the Rio Grande or in that of the Colorado River, in that portion thereof wherein those rivers form the boundary line between the two countries, which may affect the boundary line, notice of that fact shall be given by the proper local authorities on both sides to their respective commissioners of the International Boundary Commission, on receiving which notice it shall be the duty of the said Commission to repair to the place where the change has taken place or the question has arisen, to make a personal examination of such change, to compare it with the bed of the river as it was before the change took place, as shown by the surveys, and to decide whether it has occurred through avulsion or erosion, for the effects of Articles 1 and 2 of the convention of November 12th, 1884; having done this, it shall make suitable annotations on the surveys of the boundary line.

VI

CONVENTION BETWEEN THE UNITED STATES AND MEXICO FOR THE
ELIMINATION OF THE BANCOS IN THE RIO GRANDE FROM THE EFFECTS OF
ARTICLE II OF THE TREATY OF NOVEMBER 12, 1884.

Signed at Washington March 20, 1905; ratification advised by the Senate February 28, 1907; ratified by the President of the United States March 13, 1907; ratifications exchanged May 31, 1907; proclaimed June 5, 1907.

Whereas, for the purpose of obviating the difficulties arising from the application of Article 5 of the treaty of Guadalupe Hidalgo, dated February 2, 1848, and Article 1 of the treaty of December 30, 1853, both concluded between the United States of America and Mexico — difficulties growing out of the frequent changes to which the beds of the Rio Grande and Colorado River are subject — there was signed in Washington on November 12, 1884, by the Plenipotentiaries of the United States and Mexico, a convention containing the following stipulations:

ARTICLE 1. — The dividing line shall forever be that described in the aforesaid treaty and follow the center of the normal channel of the rivers named, notwithstanding any alterations in the banks or in the course of those rivers, provided that such alterations be effected by natural causes through the slow and gradual erosion and deposit of alluvium and not by the abandonment of an existing river bed and the opening of a new one.

ARTICLE 2. — Any other change, wrought by the force of the current whether by the cutting of a new bed, or when there is more than one channel by the deepening of another channel than that which marked the boundary at the time of the survey made under the aforesaid treaty, shall produce no change in the dividing line as fixed by the surveys of the International Boundary Commissions in 1852, but the line then fixed shall continue to follow the middle of the original channel bed, even though this should become wholly dry or be obstructed by deposits.

Whereas, as a result of the topographical labors of the Boundary Commission created by the convention of March 1, 1889, it has been observed that there is a typical class of changes effected in the bed of the Rio Grande, in which, owing to slow and gradual erosion, coupled with avulsion, said river abandons its old channel and there are separated from it small portions of land known as *"bancos"* bounded by the said old bed, and which, according to the terms of Article 2 of the aforementioned convention of 1884, remain subject to the dominion and jurisdiction of the country from which they have been separated;

Whereas, said *"bancos"* are left at a distance from the new river bed, and by reason of the successive deposits of alluvium, the old channel is becoming effaced, the land of said *"bancos"* becomes confused with the land of the *"bancos"* contiguous thereto, thus giving rise to difficulties and controversies, some of an international and others of a private character;

Whereas, the labors of the International Boundary Commission, undertaken with the object of fixing the boundary line with reference to the *"bancos,"* have demonstrated that the application to these *"bancos"* of the principle established in Article 2 of the convention of 1884 renders difficult the solution of the controversies mentioned, and, instead of simplifying, complicates the said boundary line between the two countries;

Therefore, the Governments of the United States of America and the United States of Mexico, being desirous to enter into a convention to establish more fitting rules for the solution of such difficulties, have appointed as their plenipotentiaries —

That of the United States of America, Alvey A. Adee, Acting Secretary of State of the United States;

That of the United States of Mexico, its Ambassador Extraordinary and Plenipotentiary, Licenciado Don Manuel de Azpiroz;

Who, after exhibiting their full powers, found to be in good and due form, have agreed to the following articles:

ARTICLE 1

The fifty-eight (58) *bancos* surveyed and described in the report of the consulting engineers, dated May 30, 1898, to which reference is made in the record of proceedings of the International Boundary Commission, dated June 14, 1898, and which are drawn on fifty-four (54) maps on a scale of one to five thousands (1 to 5,000), and three index maps, signed by the commissioners and by the plenipotentiaries appointed by the convention, are hereby eliminated from the effects of Article 2 of the treaty of November 12, 1884.

Within the part of the Rio Grande comprised between its mouth and its confluence with the San Juan River the boundary line between the two countries shall be the broken red line shown on the said maps — that is, it shall follow the deepest channel of the stream — and the dominion and jurisdiction of so many of the aforesaid fifty-eight (58) *bancos* as may remain on the right bank of the river shall pass to Mexico, and the dominion and jurisdiction of the said fifty-eight (58) *bancos* which may remain on the left bank shall pass to the United States of America.

ARTICLE 2

The International Commission shall, in the future, be guided by the principle of elimination of the *bancos* established in the foregoing article, with regard to the labors concerning the boundary line throughout that part of the Rio Grande and the Colorado River which serves as a boundary between the two nations. There are hereby excepted from this provision the portions of land segregated by the change in the bed of the said rivers having an area of over two hundred and fifty (250) hectares, or a population of over two hundred (200) souls, and which shall not be considered as *bancos* for the purposes of this treaty and shall not be eliminated, the old bed of the river remaining, therefore, the boundary in such cases.

ARTICLE 3

With regard to the *bancos* which may be formed in future, as well as to those already formed but which are not yet surveyed, the Boundary Commission shall proceed to the places where they have been formed, for the purpose of duly applying Articles 1 and 2 of the present convention, and the proper maps shall be prepared in which the changes that have occurred shall be shown, in a manner similar to that employed in the preparation of the maps of the aforementioned fifty-eight (58) *bancos*.

As regards these *bancos,* as well as those already formed but not surveyed, and those that may be formed in future, the Commission shall mark on the ground, with suitable monuments, the bed abandoned by the river, so that the boundaries of the *bancos* shall be clearly defined.

On all separated land on which the successive alluvium deposits have caused to disappear those parts of the abandoned channel which are adjacent to the river, each of the extremities of said channel shall be united by means of a straight line to the nearest part of the bank of the same river.

VII

CONVENTION BETWEEN THE UNITED STATES OF AMERICA AND MEXICO. RECTIFICATION OF THE RIO GRANDE.

Signed at Mexico City, February 1, 1933; ratification advised by the Senate of the United States, with amendment, April 25, 1933; ratified by the President, October 20, 1933; ratifications exchanged at Washington, November 10, 1933; proclaimed, November 13, 1933.

The United States of America and the United Mexican States having taken into consideration the studies and engineering plans carried on by the International Boundary Commission, and specially directed to relieve the towns and agricultural lands located within the El Paso-Juarez Valley from flood dangers, and securing at the same time the stabilization of the international boundary line, which, owing to the present meandering nature of the river it has not been possible to hold within the mean line of its channel; and fully conscious of the great importance involved in this matter, both from a local point of view as well as from a good international understanding, have resolved to undertake, in common agreement and cooperation, the necessary works as provided in Minute 129 (dated July 31, 1930) of the International Boundary Commission, approved by the two Governments in the manner provided by treaty; and in order to give legal and final form to the project, have named as their plenipotentiaries:

The President of the United States of America, J. Reuben Clark, Jr., Ambassador Extraordinary and Plenipotentiary of the United States of America to Mexico; and

The President of the United Mexican States, Doctor Jose Manuel Puig Cassauranc, Secretary of State for Foreign Affairs;

Who, after having communicated their respective full powers and having found them in due and proper form, have agreed on the following articles:

ARTICLE 1

The Government of the United States of America and the Government of the United Mexican States have agreed to carry out the Rio Grande rectification works provided for in Minute 129 of the International Boundary Commission and annexes thereto, approved by both Governments, in that part of the river beginning at the point of intersection of the present river channel with the locate line as shown in map, exhibit No. 2 of Minute 129 of said Commission (said intersection being south of Monument 15 of the boundary polygon of Cordoba Island) and ending at Box Canyon.

The terms of this Convention and of Minute 129 shall apply exclusively to river rectification within the limits above set out.

The two Governments shall study such further minutes and regulations as may be submitted by the International Boundary Commission and, finding them acceptable, shall approve same in order to carry out the material execution of the works in accordance with the terms of this Convention. The works shall be begun after this Convention becomes effective.

ARTICLE 5

The International Boundary Commission shall survey the ground to be used as the right of way to be occupied by the rectified channel, as well as the parts to be cut from both sides of said channel. Within thirty days after a cut has been made, it shall mark the boundaries on the ground, there being a strict superficial compensation in total of the areas taken from each country. Once the corresponding maps have been prepared, the Commission shall eliminate these areas from the provisions of Article II of the Convention of November 12, 1884, in similar manner to that adopted in the Convention of March 20, 1905 for the elimination of bancos.

ARTICLE 6

For the sole purpose of equalizing areas, the axis of the rectified channel shall be the international boundary line. The parcels of land that, as a result of these cuts or of merely taking the new axis of the channel as the boundary line, shall remain on the American side of the axis of the rectified channel shall be the territory and property of the United States of America, and the territory and property of the United Mexican States those on the opposite side, each Government mutually surrendering in favor of the other the acquired rights over such parcels.

In the completed rectified river channel — both in its normal and constructed sections — and in any completed portion thereof, the permanent international boundary shall be the middle of the deepest channel of the river within such rectified river channel.

VIII

CONVENTION BETWEEN THE UNITED STATES OF AMERICA AND THE UNITED MEXICAN STATES FOR THE SOLUTION OF THE PROBLEM OF THE CHAMIZAL

Convention signed at Mexico City August 29, 1963; ratification advised by

the Senate of the United States of America December 17, 1963; ratified by the President of the United States of America December 20, 1963; ratified by Mexico January 7, 1964; ratifications exchanged at Mexico City January 14, 1964; proclaimed by the President of the United States of America January 16, 1964; entered into force January 14, 1964. With exchange of notes signed at Mexico City August 29, 1963.

The United States of America and the United Mexican States:

Animated by the spirit of good neighborliness which has made possible the amicable solution of various problems which have arisen between them;

Desiring to arrive at a complete solution of the problem concerning El Chamizal, an area of land situated to the north of the Rio Grande, in the El Paso-Ciudad Juarez region;

Considering that the recommendations of the Department of State of the United States and the Ministry of Foreign Relations of Mexico of July 17, 1963, have been approved by the Presidents of the two Republics;

Desiring to give effect to the 1911 arbitration award in today's circumstances and in keeping with the joint communique of the Presidents of the United States and of Mexico issued on June 30, 1962; and

Convinced of the need for continuing the program of rectification and stabilization of the Rio Grande which has been carried out under the terms of the Convention of February 1, 1933, by improving the channel in the El Paso-Ciudad Juarez region,

Have resolved to conclude a Convention and for this purpose have named as their Plenipotentiaries:

The President of the United States of America, Thomas C. Mann, Ambassador of the United States of America to Mexico, and

The President of the United Mexican States, Manuel Tello, Secretary for Foreign Relations.

Who, having communicated to each other their respective Full Powers, found to be in good and due form, have agreed as follows:

ARTICLE 1

In the El Paso-Ciudad Juarez sector, the Rio Grande shall be relocated into a new channel in accordance with the engineering plan recommended in Minute No. 214 of the International Boundary and Water Commission, United States and Mexico. Authentic copies of the Minute and of the map attached thereto, on which the new channel is shown, are annexed to this Convention and made a part hereof.

ARTICLE 2

The river channel shall be relocated so as to transfer from the north to the south of the Rio Grande a tract of 823.50 acres composed of 366.00 acres in the Chamizal tract, 193.16 acres in the southern part of Cordova Island, and 264.34 acres to the east of Cordova Island. A tract of 193.16 acres in the northern part of Cordova Island will remain to the north of the river.

ARTICLE 3

The center line of the new river channel shall be the international boundary. The lands that, as a result of the relocation of the river channel, shall be to the north of the center line of the new channel shall be the territory of the United States of America and the lands that shall be to the south of the center line of the new channel shall be the territory of the United Mexican States.

ARTICLE 7

As soon as the operations provided in the preceding article have been completed, and the payment made by the Banco Nacional Hipotecario Urbano y de Obras Publicas, S.A., to the Government of the United States as provided in Article 5, the Government of the United States shall so inform the Government of Mexico. The International Boundary and Water Commission shall then proceed to demarcate the new international boundary, recording the demarcation in a Minute. The relocation of the international boundary and the transfer of lands provided for in this Convention shall take place upon express approval of that Minute by both Governments in accordance with the procedure established in the second paragraph of Article 25 of the Treaty of February 3, 1944.

IX

TREATY TO RESOLVE PENDING BOUNDARY DIFFERENCES AND MAINTAIN THE RIO GRANDE AND COLORADO RIVER AS THE INTERNATIONAL BOUNDARY BETWEEN THE UNITED STATES OF AMERICA AND THE UNITED MEXICAN STATES

Signed at Mexico City on November 23, 1970.

The United States of America and the United Mexican States,
Animated by a spirit of close friendship and mutual respect and desiring to:

Resolve all pending boundary differences between the two countries,
Restore to the Rio Grande its character of international boundary in the reaches where that character has been lost, and preserve for the Rio Grande and Colorado River the character of international boundaries ascribed to them by the boundary treaties in force,
Minimize changes in the channels of these rivers, and should these

changes occur, attempt to resolve the problems arising therefrom promptly and equitably,

Resolve problems relating to sovereignty over existing or future islands in the Rio Grande,

And finally, considering that it is in the interest of both countries to delimit clearly their maritime boundaries in the Gulf of Mexico and in the Pacific Ocean,

Have resolved to conclude this Treaty concerning their fluvial and maritime boundaries and for such purpose have named their plenipotentiaries:

The President of the United States of America, Robert H. McBride, Ambassador of the United States of America to Mexico, and

The President of the United Mexican States, Antonio Carrillo Flores, Secretary of Foreign Relations,

Who, having communicated to each other their respective full powers, found to be in good and due form, have agreed as follows:

ARTICLE 1

In order to resolve the pending boundary cases of the Presidio-Ojinaga Tracts, the Horcon Tract, Beaver Island, and islands, in which the territory of one of the Contracting States has been placed on the opposite bank of the Rio Grande, and to restore this river as the international boundary, the United States and Mexico have decided to modify the position of the Rio Grande in certain reaches, in accordance with the following terms:

A. To change the location of a section of the channel of the Rio Grande in the area of the Presidio-Ojinaga Tracts, so as to transfer from the north to the south side of the Rio Grande an area of 1606.19 acres (650 hectares). This relocation shall be effected so that the middle of the new channel follows the alignment shown on the map of the International Boundary and Water Commission, United States and Mexico (hereinafter referred to as the "Commission"), entitled Relocation of the Rio Grande in the Presidio-Ojinaga Tracts, attached to and forming a part of this Treaty.

B. To change the location of the channel of the Rio Grande upstream from and near Hidalgo-Reynosa, so as to transfer from the south to the north of the Rio Grande an area of 481.68 acres (194.93 hectares). This relocation shall be effected so that the middle of the rectified channel follows the alignment shown on the Commission's map entitled Relocation of the Rio Grande Upstream from Hidalgo-Reynosa, attached to and forming a part of this Treaty.

C. To change the location of the channel of the Rio Grande downstream from and near Presidio-Ojinaga, so as to transfer from the south to the north of the Rio Grande an area of 252 acres (101.98 hectares). This relocation shall be effected so that the middle of the rectified channel follows the alignment shown on the Commission's map entitled Relocation of the Rio Grande Downstream from Presidio-Ojinaga, attached to and forming a part of this Treaty.

D. Once this Treaty has come into force and the necessary legislation has been enacted for carrying it out, the two Governments shall determine, on the basis of a recommendation by the Commission, the period of time appropriate for each of them to carry out the following operations:

(1) The acquisition, in conformity with its laws, of the lands to be transferred to the other and of the rights of way for the new river channels;

(2) The orderly evacuation of the occupants of the lands referred to in paragraph D (1) of this Article.

E. The changes in location of the Rio Grande referred to in paragraphs A, B and C of this Article, shall be executed by the Commission as soon as practical in accordance with the engineering plans recommended by it and approved by the two Governments. The cost of these changes in location shall be equally divided between the two Governments, through an appropriate division of work recommended by the Commission in the same engineering plans.

F. On the date on which the two Governments approve the Commission's Minute confirming the completion of the relocations of the channel of the Rio Grande provided for in paragraphs A, B and C of this Article, the change of location of the international boundary shall be effected in each case and the middle of the new channels of the Rio Grande and of the present channels north of the Horcon Tract and north of Beaver Island shall become the international boundary; and consequently the following territorial adjustments shall take place:

(1) By reason of the rectification referred to in paragraph A of this Article, there shall pass from the north to the south of the Rio Grande within the territory of Mexico, 1606.19 acres (650 hectares) in the Presidio-Ojinaga Tracts.

(2) By reason of the rectification referred to in paragraph B of this Article, there shall pass from the south to the north of the Rio Grande 481.-68 acres (194.93 hectares) to form a part of the territory of the United States. This transfer is in recognition of the fact that the Horcon Tract and Beaver Island, located south of the Rio Grande, comprising a total area of 481.68 acres (194.93 hectares) now under the sovereignty of the United States shall pass to and become part of the territory of Mexico.

(3) By reason of the rectification referred to in paragraph C of this Article, there shall pass from the south to the north of the Rio Grande 252 acres (101.98 hectares) to form a part of the territory of the United States. This transfer is in recognition of the fact that, upon the adoption of the new boundary in accordance with Article II of this Treaty, Mexico will

receive a greater number and acreage of islands than the United States.

ARTICLE 2

In order to resolve uncertainties relating to the sovereignty over islands and to restore to the Rio Grande its character as the international boundary in those locations where this character has been lost between the Gulf of Mexico and its intersection with the land boundary, the Contracting States agree that:

A. Except as provided in Articles I (F), III (B) and III (C) of this Treaty, from the date on which this Treaty enters into force, the international boundary between the United States and Mexico in the limitrophe sections of the Rio Grande and the Colorado River shall run along the middle of the channel occupied by normal flow and, where either of the rivers has two or more channels, along the middle of the channel which in normal flows has the greater or greatest average width over its length, and from that time forward, this international boundary shall determine the sovereignty over the lands on one side or the other of it, regardless of the previous sovereignty over these lands.

B. For the purposes of this Treaty, the Commission shall in each case determine the normal flows, which shall exclude flood flows, and the average widths, referred to in the preceding paragraph of this Article.

C. The Commission, on the basis of the surveys which it shall carry out as soon as practical, shall with appropriate precision delineate the international boundary on maps or aerial photographic mosaics of the Rio Grande and of the Colorado River. In the future, the Commission shall make surveys as frequently as it may consider justifiable, but in any event at intervals of not greater than ten years, and shall record the position of the international boundary on appropriate maps. Each of the Governments shall bear half of the costs and other expenses determined by the Commission and approved by the two Governments for the surveys and maps relating to the boundaries.

ARTICLE 3

In order to minimize problems brought about by future changes in the limitrophe channels of the Rio Grande and the Colorado River, the Contracting States agree that:

A. When the Rio Grande or the Colorado River moves laterally eroding one of its banks and depositing alluvium on the opposite bank, the international boundary shall continue to follow the middle of the channel occupied by normal flow or, where there are two or more channels, it shall follow the middle of the channel which in normal flow has the greatest average width over its length.

B. (1) When the Rio Grande or the Colorado River, through movements other than those described in paragraph A of this Article, separates from one Contracting State a tract of land, which might be composed of or include islands, of no more than 617.76 acres (250 hectares) and with an established population of no more than 100 inhabitants, the Contracting State from which the tract of land has been separated shall have the right to restore the river to its prior position and shall notify the other Contracting State, through the Commission, at the earliest possible date whether or not it proposes to restore the river to its prior position. Such restoration must be made at its own expense within a period of three years counted from the date on which the Commission acknowledges the separation; however, if such restoration should have been initiated but not completed within the period of three years, the Commission, with approval of both Governments, may extend it for one year. The boundary shall remain in its prior location during the periods herein provided for restoration of the river, notwithstanding the provisions of Article II (A) of this Treaty.

(2) If at the conclusion of the periods herein provided the river has not been restored to its prior position, the international boundary shall be fixed in accordance with the provisions of Article II (A) of this Treaty, and sovereignty over the separated tract of land shall, as of that date, pass to the Contracting State on whose side of the river the separated tract is then located. Should the Contracting State from whose territory the tract was separated notify the other Contracting State of its intention not to restore the river to its prior position, the international boundary shall be fixed in accordance with the provisions of Article II (A) of this Treaty, and sovereignty over the separated tract shall change as of the date on which notification is given through the Commission.

(3) When a tract of land passes from the sovereignty of one Contracting State to the other in accordance with paragraph B (2) of this Article, its area shall be ascertained and recorded by the Commission as a credit in favor of the Contracting State from which it was separated, for later compensation by an equal area in a natural separation of a tract of the other Contracting State which is not restored or in a future rectification recommended by the Commission and approved by the two Governments in the same river. The costs of such rectifications shall be divided equally between the Contracting States and, upon completion, the middle of the new channels shall become the international boundary and the Commission shall cancel the corresponding credit.

C. When the Rio Grande or the Colorado River, by movements other than those provided in paragraph A of this Article, separates from one Contracting State a tract of land, which might be composed of or include islands, having an area of more than 617.76 acres (250 hectares) or an established population of more than 100 inhabitants, the international boundary shall remain in its prior position and sovereignty over the separated tract of land shall not change, notwithstanding the provisions of Article II (A) of this Treaty. In such cases the Commission shall restore the river to its prior channel as soon as practical, equally dividing the costs between the Contracting States. As an alternative procedure the Commission, with the approval of the two Governments, may rectify the channel of the river in the same section in which the separation occurred, so as to transfer an equal area to the Contracting State from which the tract of land was separated. The costs of these rectifications shall be divided equally between the two Governments and upon their completion, the middle of the new channels shall be the international boundary, as defined in Article II (A) of this Treaty.

D. The Commissioners shall exchange all information coming to their attention about possible or actual separation of lands as referred to in paragraphs B and C of this Article. The Commission shall promptly make the necessary surveys and investigations in all cases of separation and determine, in accordance with the provisions of paragraphs B and C of this Article, which type of separation has taken place.

E. Pending any changes in sovereignty brought about by the application of paragraphs B or C of this Article, each Contracting State shall extend to the nationals of the other such facilities for transit through its territory as may be necessary to permit the use and enjoyment of separated tracts as before the separation, including such exemption from customs duties and immigration procedures as may be necessary.

F. When in the limitrophe reaches of the Rio Grande and Colorado River, a part of the channel temporarily loses its character as the boundary by reason of the changes contemplated in paragraphs B and C of this Article, the international character of the use and consumption of those waters, in the order established under Article 3 of the Treaty of February 3, 1944, shall not be modified.

ARTICLE 5

The Contracting States agree to establish and recognize their maritime boundaries in the Gulf of Mexico and in the Pacific Ocean in accordance with the following provisions:

A. The international maritime boundary in the Gulf of Mexico shall begin at the center of the mouth of the Rio Grande, wherever it may be located; from there it shall run in a straight line to a fixed point, at 25 deg. 57 min. 22.18 sec. North latitude, and 97 deg. 8 min. 19.76 sec. West longitude, situated approximately 2,000 feet seaward from the coast; from this fixed point the maritime boundary shall continue seaward in a straight line the delineation of which represents a practical simplification of the line drawn in accordance with the principle of equidistance established in Article 12 and 24 of the Geneva Convention on the Territorial Sea and the Contiguous Zone. This line shall extend into the Gulf of Mexico to a distance of 12 nautical miles from the baseline used for its delineation. The international maritime boundary in the Gulf of Mexico shall be recognized in accordance with the map entitled International Maritime Boundary in the Gulf of Mexico, which the Commission shall prepare in conformity with the foregoing description and which, once approved by the Governments, shall be annexed to and form part of this Treaty.

B. The international maritime boundary in the Pacific Ocean shall begin at the westernmost point of the mainland boundary; from there it shall run seaward on a line the delineation of which represents a practical simplification, through a series of straight lines, of the line drawn in accordance with the principle of equidistance established in Articles 12 and 24 of the Geneva Convention on the Territorial Sea and the Contiguous Zone. This line shall extend seaward to a distance of 12 nautical miles from the baselines used for its delineation along the coast of the mainland and the islands of the Contracting States. The international maritime boundary in the Pacific Ocean shall be recognized in accordance with the map entitled International Maritime Boundary in the Pacific Ocean, which the Commission shall prepare in conformity with the foregoing description and which, once approved by the Governments, shall be annexed to and form a part of this Treaty.

C. These maritime boundaries, as they are shown in maps of the Commission entitled International Maritime Boundary in the Gulf of Mexico and International Maritime Boundary in the Pacific Ocean, shall be recognized as of the date on which this Treaty enters into force. They shall permanently represent the maritime boundaries between the two Contracting States; on the south side of these boundaries the United States shall not, and on the north side of them Mexico shall not, for any purpose claim or exercise sovereignty, sovereign rights or jurisdiction over the waters, air space, or seabed and subsoil. Once recognized, these new boundaries shall supersede the provisional maritime boundaries referred to in the Commission's Minute No. 229.

D. The establishment of these new maritime boundaries shall not affect or prejudice in any manner the positions of either of the Contracting States with respect to the extent of internal waters, of the territorial sea, or of sovereign rights or jurisdiction for any other purpose.

E. The Commission shall recommend the means of physically marking the maritime boundaries and of the division of work for construction and maintenance of the markers. When such recommendations have been approved by the two Governments the Commission shall construct and maintain the markers, the cost of which shall be equally divided between the Contracting States.

BIBLIOGRAPHY

Ainsworth, C. M., and F. P. Brown. *Report on the Changes In Regimen of the Rio Grande in the Valleys Below Since the Construction of Elephant Butte Dam, 1917-1932.* Unpublished report of the United States Section, International Boundary and Water Commission, El Paso, 1933.

American Geological Institute. *Glossary of Geology.* Published by the Institute, Washington, 1960.

Baker, J. N. L. *A History of Geographical Discovery and Exploration.* George G. Harrap, London, 1937.

Baker, W. W. *The Construction of the Canalization Feature of the Rio Grande Canalization Project.* Unpublished final report of the United States Section, International Boundary and Water Commission, El Paso, 1943.

Bartlett, John R. *Personal Narrative of Explorations and Incidents in Texas, New Mexico, California, Sonora, and Chihuahua.* 2 vols. Appleton and Company, New York, 1854.

Bryan, Kirk. *Regional Planning: Part 4, The Rio Grande Joint Investigation in the Upper Rio Grande Basin in Colorado, New Mexico and Texas 1936-1937.* National Resource Commission, U.S. Government Printing Office, Washington, 1938.

Conner, Seymour. *Adventure in Glory.* Steck-Vaughn, Austin, 1965.

Cravioto G., Eduardo. *Runoff of the Conchos River at Ojinaga Under Present and Future Conditions.* Unpublished and translated report of the United States Section, International Boundary and Water Commission, El Paso, 1946.

Cushing, Caleb. "Arcifinious Boundaries." in *Opinions of the Attorneys General* VIII, Government Printing Office, Washington, 1872, pp. 175-180.

Davis, Harold E. *History of Latin America.* Ronald Press, New York, 1968.

Day, John C. *Managing the Lower Rio Grande.* Department of Geography Research Paper no. 125, University of Chicago Press, Chicago, 1970.

Douglas, Edward M. "Boundaries, Areas, Geographic Centers and Altitudes of the United States and the Several States." United States Geological Survey *Bulletin* 817, 1930.

Dufour, Charles. *The Mexican War.* Hawthorn Books, New York, 1968.

El Paso *Herald-Post*, December 28, 1971.

Emory, William H. *Report on the United States and Mexican Boundary Survey.* House of Representatives Executive Document no. 135, vol. I, 1857.

Faulk, Odie B. *A Successful Failure.* Steck-Vaughn, Austin, 1965.

Fergusson, Harvey. *Rio Grande.* William Morrow, New York, 1955.

Fiock, L. R. *Effect of the Operation of Elephant Butte Reservoir on the River through Rio Grande Project.* Unpublished report of the United States Section, International Boundary and Water Commission, El Paso, 1931.

Follett, W. W. *A Study of an Alluvial Stream*. Report of the United States Section, International Boundary and Water Commission, El Paso, 1911.

Friedkin, J. F. *A Laboratory Study of the Meanders of Alluvial Rivers*. U.S. Waterways Engineering Experiment Station, Vicksburg, 1945.

————. *A Preliminary Statement on the Unprecedented Rio Grande Flood — September, 1967*. Press release of the United States Commissioner, International Boundary and Water Commission, El Paso, 1967.

————. *Proposed Flood Control Project Rio Grande, Presidio Valley, Texas*. Unpublished report of the United States Section, International Boundary and Water Commission, El Paso, 1971.

Fullerton, Frank P. *The Implementation of the Chamizal Settlement*. Unpublished Masters Thesis, The University of Texas at El Paso, 1968.

Gile, L. H., J. W. Hawley, and R. B. Grossman. *Distribution and Genesis of Soils and Geomorphic Surfaces in a Desert Region of Southern New Mexico*. Guidebook for Soil — Geomorphology Field Conferences of the Soil Science Society of America, 1970.

Gilluly, J., A. C. Waters, and A. O. Woodford. *Principles of Geology*. W. H. Freeman, San Francisco, 1968.

Gould, Wesley L. *An Introduction to International Law*. Harper and Brothers, New York, 1957.

Gregory, Gladys. *"El Chamizal": A Boundary Problem Between the United States and Mexico*. Unpublished Ph.D. dissertation, University of Texas, Austin, 1937.

————. *The Chamizal Settlement*. Texas Western Press, El Paso, 1963.

Hackworth, Green H. *Digest of International Law*, I. Department of State, Government Printing Office, Washington, 1940.

Hamlyn, E. E., Engineer, Boundary Section, United States Section, International Boundary and Water Commission, personal communication, December 28, 1971, December 22, 1972.

Hasbrouck, Alfred. "The Movements for Independence in Mexico and Central America." *Colonial Hispanic America*. Ed. by A. Curtis Wilgus. Russell and Russell, New York, 1963.

Henderson, T. E., Technical Staff Assistant, United States Section, International Boundary and Water Commission, interview, March 13, 1974.

Herrera Jordan, David, and Joseph F. Friedkin. *The International Boundary and Water Commission United States and Mexico*. Paper read before International Conference on Water for Peace, Washington, 1967.

Horgan, Paul. *Great River*. Rinehart and Company, New York, 2 vols., 1954.

————. "Rio Grande: Odyssey From a Wintry Birth." Washington *Post*, August 9, 1970.

Hovel, John A. *The Chamizal*. Unpublished report, El Paso City Plan Commission, 1960.

Hyde, Charles C. *International Law*, I. Little, Brown and Company, Boston, 1947.

Ingle, R. M., El Paso, Texas, interview, October 14, 1971.

International Boundary and Water Commission, United States and Mexico. *Minute* 124, 1963.

Jaeger, Edmund C. *The North American Deserts*. Stanford University Press, Palo Alto, 1957.

Bibliography

James, L. L. "World's Most Expensive Guidebook." *New Mexico Magazine*, XLVIII, January, 1970, pp. 24-33.

Keeler, Karl F. *A Study of Flood Occurrences on the Rio Grande at Laredo, Texas.* Unpublished report of the United States Section, International Boundary and Water Commission, El Paso, 1956.

————. *A Study of Flood Occurrences on the Rio Grande at Amistad Dam Site Near Del Rio, Texas For the 214 Year Period 1746 through 1959.* Unpublished report of the United States Section, International Boundary and Water Commission, El Paso, 1960.

Kottlowski, Frank E. "Geological History of the Rio Grande near El Paso." *West Texas Geological Society Guidebook*, 1958 Field Trip, Franklin and Hueco Mountains, Texas, 1958, pp. 46-54.

Lawson, L. M. "Rectification of the Rio Grande." *Civil Engineering*, VII, 1937, pp. 457-461.

Leopold, Luna B., M. Gordon Wolman, and John P. Miller. *Fluvial Processes in Geomorphology.* W. H. Freeman and Company, San Francisco, 1964.

Liss, Sheldon B. *A Century of Disagreement: The Chamizal Conflict 1864-1964.* University Press, Washington, 1965.

McNealy, D. D., Executive Officer, United States Section, International Boundary and Water Commission, interview, March 12, 1974.

Maxwell, R. A., and J. N. Dietrich. "Geologic Summary of the Big Bend Region." *West Texas Geological Society Guidebook*, Geology of the Big Bend Area, Texas, 1965, pp. 11-33.

Mills, Anson. *My Story.* Byron S. Adams Press, Washington, 1921.

Monkhouse, F. J. *A Dictionary of Geography.* Aldine Publishing Company, Chicago, 1970.

Moore, J. B. *A Digest of International Law*, I. Department of State, Government Printing Office, Washington, 1906.

Moore, W. G. *A Dictionary of Geography.* Penguin Books Inc., Baltimore, 1968.

Oppenheim, L. *International Law*, II. Longmans, Green and Co., London, 1928.

Orton, Robert B. *The Climate of Texas and the Adjacent Gulf Waters.* United States Weather Bureau, Department of Commerce, 1964.

Reinhardt, G. Frederick. "Rectification of the Rio Grande in the El Paso-Juarez Valley." *American Journal of International Law*, XXXI, 1937, pp. 44-54.

Robinson, T. W. "Phreatophytes." United States Geological Survey *Water-Supply Paper* 1423, Washington, 1958.

Ruhe, Robert V. "Age of the Rio Grande Valley in Southern New Mexico." *Journal of Geology*, LXX, 1962, pp. 151-167.

Sahovic, Milan and William W. Bishop. "The Authority of the State: Its Range With Respect to Persons and Places." *Manual of Public International Law*, Ed. Max Sorensen, St. Martin's Press, New York, 1968.

Schumm, S. A. "The Shape of Alluvial Channels in Relation to Sediment Type." United States Geological Survey *Professional Paper* 352-B, 1960.

———— and R. W. Lichty. "Channel Widening and Flood-Plain Construction Along Cimarron River in Southwestern Kansas. United States Geological Survey *Professional Paper* 352-D, 1963.

Scott, Florence. *Historical Heritage of the Lower Rio Grande.* Texian Press, Waco, 1966.

Shelford, Victor E. *Ecology of North America.* University of Illinois Press, Urbana, 1963.

Sonnichsen, C. L. *Pass of the North.* Texas Western Press, El Paso, 1968.

Steen, Ralph W. *The Texas Story.* Steck Company, Austin, 1948.

Strain, William S. *Blancan Mammalian Fauna and Pleistocene Formations, Hudspeth County, Texas.* Bulletin 10, Texas Memorial Museum, Austin, 1966.

————. "Bolson Integration in the Texas-Chihuahua Border Region." Society of Economic Paleontologists and Mineralogists, *Permian Basin Section Guidebook,* Geology of South Quitman Mountains Area Trans-Pecos Texas, 1970, pp. 88-90.

Swift, Richard N. *International Law: Current and Classic.* John Wiley and Sons, New York, 1969.

Texas Water Development Board. *Engineering Data on Dams and Reservoirs in Texas.* Report 126, Part III, 1971.

Timm, Charles A. *The International Boundary Commission.* University of Texas Press, Austin, 1941.

Twain, Mark. *Life on the Mississippi.* James R. Osgood and Co., Boston, 1883.

United States and Mexico. *Treaty of Guadalupe Hidalgo.* 9 Statutes, 922, 1848.

————. *Gadsden Treaty,* 10 Statutes, 1051, 1853.

————. *Boundary Convention.* 22 Statutes, 986, 1882.

————. *Boundary Convention.* 24 Statutes, 1011, 1884.

————. *Convention to Establish the International Boundary Commission.* 26 Statutes, 1512, 1889.

————. *Banco Treaty.* 35 Statutes, 1863, 1905.

————. *Convention for Equitable Distribution of Rio Grande Water.* 34 Statutes, 2953, 1906.

————. *Convention for the Arbitration of the Chamizal Case.* 36 Statutes, 2481, 1910.

————. *Convention for Rio Grande Rectification.* 48 Statutes, 1621, 1933.

————. *Water Allocation Treaty.* 59 Statutes, 1219, 1944.

————. *Convention for the Solution of the Problem of the Chamizal.* 15 United States Treaties, 21, 1963.

————. "Treaty of 1970 Resolving Boundary Differences." *Message from the President, United States Senate, 92d Congress, 1st Session,* Government Printing Office, Washington, 1971.

United States Department of Commerce. *Local Climatological Data, Brownsville, Texas.* Government Printing Office, Washington, 1970a.

————. *Local Climatological Data, Del Rio, Texas.* Government Printing Office, Washington, 1970b.

————. *Local Climatological Data, El Paso, Texas.* Government Printing Office, Washington, 1970c.

————. *1970 Census of Population, Texas.* United States Bureau of the Census: Government Printing Office, Washington, 1971-72.

United States Department of State. *Proceedings of the International (Water) Boundary Commission I.* Government Printing Office, Washington, 1903.

Bibliography

————. *Elimination of Bancos.* First Series, nos. 1-58, Government Printing Office, Washington, 1910.

————. *Chamizal Arbitration: Appendix to the Case of the United States.* Government Printing Office, Washington, 2 vols., 1911.

————. *Chamizal Arbitration: Argument of the United States of America.* Government Printing Office, Washington, 1911.

————. *Chamizal Arbitration: Award in the Chamizal Case.* Government Printing Office, Washington, 1911.

————. *Chamizal Arbitration: Case of the United States of America and Portfolio of Maps.* Government Printing Office, Washington, 1911.

————. *Chamizal Arbitration: Countercase of the United States of America.* Government Printing Office, Washington, 1911.

————. *Elimination of Bancos.* Second Series, nos. 59-89, Government Printing Office, Washington, 1911.

————. "Mexico." in *Foreign Relations of the United States.* Government Printing Office, Washington, 1911.

————. *Department of State Bulletin,* XLIX. Government Printing Office, Washington, 1963.

United States Section, International Boundary and Water Commission, "Flow of the Rio Grande and Related Data." *Water Bulletins* published annually since 1932, El Paso, Texas.

————. *Report on Flood Control Investigation Central Section Presidio Valley.* Unpublished report, El Paso, 1940.

————. *History and Development of the International Boundary and Water Commission.* Unpublished report (rev.), El Paso, 1954.

————. *Flood of September,* 1968. Unpublished report, El Paso, 1969.

Utley, Robert M. *The International Boundary.* National Park Service, Southwest Region, Santa Fe, 1964.

Vandertulip, J. J., Chief, Planning and Reports, United States Section, International Boundary and Water Commission, interview, March 13, 1974.

Van Zandt, Franklin K. "Boundaries of the United States and the Several States." United States Geological Survey *Bulletin* 1212, 1966.

Worthington, R. D., Department of Biological Sciences, University of Texas at El Paso, personal communication, September 22, 1972.

ACKNOWLEDGEMENTS

ACKNOWLEDGEMENT IS GIVEN to Dr. M. Gordon Wolman and Professor Charles B. Hunt of the Johns Hopkins University for their valuable advice and constructive criticisms throughout the preparation of this book. The author also expresses his gratitude to Drs. George H. Dury of the University of Wisconsin and Virgil R. Baker of Arizona State University for their thorough reviews of the manuscript and for their excellent suggestions for improving the mechanical aspects of the text. Thanks also to Drs. Lewis F. Hatch, John M. Hills, Earl M. P. Lovejoy, W. N. McAnulty, and William S. Strain for the encouragement and courtesies afforded the author during his 1970-73 appointment at the University of Texas at El Paso. Dr. Richard G. Reider of the University of Wyoming contributed several helpful suggestions which were incorporated into the final draft of the manuscript.

Special appreciation is extended to the United States Section of the International Boundary and Water Commission for providing access to its excellent library, for supplying previously unpublished data, and for furnishing the photographs in Figures VIII-1, IX-1, IX-3, X-1, X-3. Ambassador Joseph F. Friedkin, Commissioner of the United States Section, also reviewed the manuscript and offered valuable suggestions for improvement. The assistance of Ted Apley in all phases of the illustrative work is appreciated. Finally, the author acknowledges those persons who assisted in typing the manuscript, including Patti Young, Bonnie Joerschke, and his wife, Bunny.

INDEX

Index

St. Croix, River, Maine — New Brunswick, 32
St. John River, Maine — New Brunswick, 32
Salazar, Major, 22, 23, 27, 37, 43, 51, 65, 67, 70, 105
Sanchez, Francisco (Chamuscado), 10
San Diego, California, 22, 24
San Elizario, Island of, 75
San Elizario, Texas, 25, 83, 84
San Jacinto, Texas, 17
San Juan Mountains, Colorado, 1
Santa Anna, Antonio Lopez de, 16-18
Santa Rita, New Mexico, 24
Scott, Winfield, 18
Selden Canyon, 90
Seward, William H., 39
Sierra Madre, 26
Socorro, Texas, 11
Sonoran Desert, 6
Sosa, Gaspar Castano de, 11
Spanish Revolution, 16
Stockton Plateau, 1

Tamarisk (saltcedar), 85, 88
Taylor, Zachary, 18, 22
Tellez, Manuel C., 75
Thalweg, Principle of, 19, 31, 32, 37, 40
Tiguas, 11
Tijuana, Baha California, 46
Tower, John, 103
Treaty,
of 1842 (Webster — Ashburton), 32
of 1848 (Guadalupe Hidalgo), 19, 21, 27, 38-40, 43, 44, 70, 113, 121, 128, 129
of 1853 (Gadsden Purchase), 26, 43, 70, 113, 121, 129, 130
of 1882 (Boundary Convention), 43, 131, 132
of 1884 (Morteritos), 40-45, 49, 50, 53, 54, 65-67, 70-73, 109, 110, 113, 115, 124, 132, 133

of 1889 (Boundary Commission), 44, 45, 54, 66, 113, 133, 134
of 1905 (Banco Convention), 46, 53-58, 63, 64, 77, 88, 103, 105, 109, 112-114, 122, 124, 134-137
of 1906 (Water Allocation), 77, 90, 124
of 1910 (Chamizal Arbitration), 69, 72, 73
of 1933 (Rectification), 75, 86, 88, 89, 99, 103, 113, 114, 124, 137, 138
of 1944 (International Waters), 94, 124
of 1963 (Chamizal Settlement), 99, 101-103, 114, 124, 138-140
of 1970 (Boundary Convention), 64, 105, 107, 109, 110, 112-115, 119, 120, 122, 123, 125, 140-147
of Luneville (1801), 32
Trevino, Don Anastacio, 60
Truman, Harry S., 99
Turk, 10
Turner, Josiah, 60, 61
Twain, Mark, 118

United States Canal, 82
United States Geological Survey, 119
Upper Presidio Gaging Station, 90, 91, 119

Veracruz, Veracruz, 8, 9, 16, 18

Weller, John, 22
Wharf Company, 39
Whipple, Lieutenant, 23, 24
Wilson, T. F., 39
Wilson, Woodrow, 75

Ysleta Mission, 11

Zuni Pueblo, 10